THE CROSSING

By

Roy Thomas Montz

Paperback ISBN: 978-1-966606-12-3

Hardcover ISBN: 978-1-966606-13-0

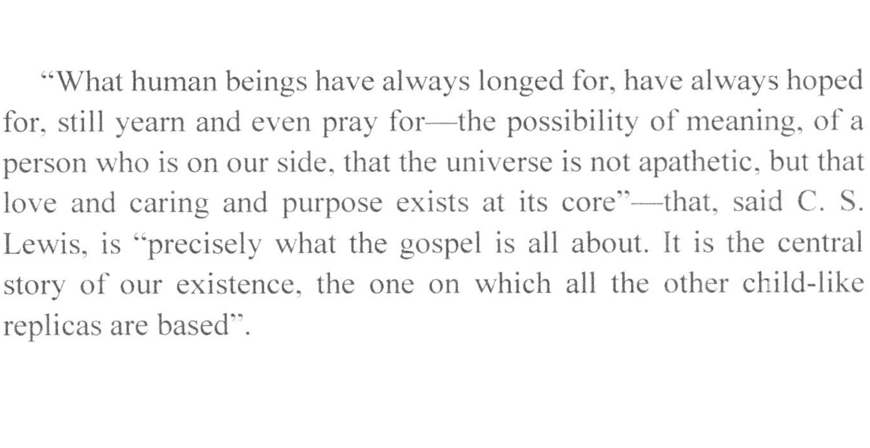

"What human beings have always longed for, have always hoped for, still yearn and even pray for—the possibility of meaning, of a person who is on our side, that the universe is not apathetic, but that love and caring and purpose exists at its core"—that, said C. S. Lewis, is "precisely what the gospel is all about. It is the central story of our existence, the one on which all the other child-like replicas are based".

CONTENTS

PROLOGUE

This is a totally fictional account of an attempt to swim across the Mississippi River at Ama, Louisiana. On a dare, as a freshman in high school, I set out to swim across the 1,200-foot-wide river. After only a few minutes in the water, and before I reached the main channel where the current was strongest, I had an epiphany. I realized the insanity of the effort and turned back toward the west bank, from where I had begun the aborted journey. The teenager who returned to that muddy bank was a great deal wiser—and far more humbled—than the boy who had first entered the water. Had I not turned back, I am certain this story would have remained untold.

I often think about what might have happened had I not made the right decision just 25 yards from the west bank. I wonder what would have become of me at 15 years old—having had my manhood challenged and arrogant enough to believe I could compete with the river for the imagined honors such an accomplishment might provide. This is a story of what might have been had I continued.

That is the message I want to communicate in this prologue. Swimming across any body of water is inherently dangerous and should always be approached with caution. But swimming across the Mississippi River is something else entirely. It is not just dangerous—it is suicidal. This story stands as a testament to a rare moment of better judgment and a way of thanking the good Lord above for helping me realize—just 25 yards out—that humility is an essential part of living and infinitely more important than imagined glory.

THE CROSSING
DATE: SEPTEMBER 8, 1937

CHAPTER 1

LOUISIANA 1935-1937

In 1937, the entire state of Louisiana was still living in the long, painful shadow cast by the death of one of its most polarizing and unforgettable figures—Senator Huey Pierce Long, known far and wide as the Kingfish. It had been two years since the fatal shooting inside the Louisiana State Capitol Building, but the pain had not dulled. The trauma, the disbelief, and the vacuum left behind by Long's sudden departure still weighed heavily on the people, especially in towns like mine, where his promises had stirred real hope.

The memory of that September afternoon in Baton Rouge remained sharp, as if time had only paused, not passed. People continued to speak about him in the present tense as if he might somehow reappear and pick up right where he left off. His name floated through churches, barber shops, feed stores, and front porches with the same reverence usually reserved for prophets. Even two years later, it wasn't uncommon to overhear conversations that circled back to that day, as though repeating it would somehow unlock a different outcome.

More than 200,000 people had attended Huey Long's funeral. The scale of that turnout was hard to comprehend, even for those of us who had come to expect the extraordinary from him. His body was laid to rest on the very grounds of the Capitol—a building he had imagined and then willed into existence. In the years since, there has been constant talk about a statue being erected at his grave. It wasn't just political chatter. It was personal for many. They needed something to cling to, something permanent that said he had been real and that he had mattered.

The conversations didn't fade with time. If anything, they became part of daily life. Whether in the kitchens of small homes or under the massive oak trees that shaded the towns and parishes, people speculated about what might have been. And while the accents changed depending on where you were—French Creole in New Orleans, a more clipped drawl in Shreveport, or a German-Cajun blend here in St. Charles Parish—the message was always the same. The people believed they had lost their one real chance.

Among Louisiana's working poor, the loss cut even deeper. These were the men and women who had nothing to begin with and saw in Long someone who understood that. He didn't just make speeches. He gave them something they could imagine. He gave them a version of life where their children could learn in real schools, where doctors could treat the sick without charity being the only payment. He told them they mattered, and in return, they gave him their loyalty, their admiration, and, in many cases, their hearts.

Those dreams didn't vanish when Long died. Instead, they hung in the air like the thick summer heat—felt by everyone, spoken of often, and impossible to ignore. There were imagined roads stretching across rural Louisiana that had never been built. Bridges that might have made once-isolated places feel connected. Schools that remained closed but whose doors, in people's minds, had already been opened. Hospital wings that had never existed but that mothers still hoped might one day serve their children. There were refineries, factories, and sugar mills that never left the drawing board. And still, the people believed these things might have become real if only Huey Long had lived just a little longer.

He had already proven what he could do—Long served two aggressive, highly active terms as Governor before moving on to the U.S. Senate. His "Share the Wealth" platform was more than a campaign slogan. It was a lifeline for people who had spent generations being ignored. He introduced bold policies that didn't just challenge the political elite. They threatened them. His reach extended far beyond Louisiana. He captured the attention of Americans from all corners of the country and rattled the nerves of Democratic Party leaders who didn't know what to make of him—or how to stop him.

He was a man people loved or hated but rarely ignored. His energy was unmatched, and his speeches were unforgettable. He could command a crowd and dominate a headline. Even small things—like promoting "pot liquor," a humble Southern broth—became symbols of his ability to connect with everyday people and turn culture into politics. He was many things at once: a visionary, a populist, a tactician, a thorn in the side of the establishment.

His ultimate goal was as enormous as it was straightforward. He wanted to make Louisiana a place where poverty wasn't a birthright. And then, he wanted to take that model to the national stage. He was determined to run for President. Many believed he could have won. His momentum was building. His followers were growing. The country was listening.

That came to a halt when a young doctor named Carl Weiss confronted him in the Capitol Building and, according to the official report, shot him in the chest. Huey Long clung to life for thirty-one hours before he died. It was a hot day in September, the kind of heat that stuck to your skin and made every hour feel longer. And with that final breath, the dream so many believed in faded into what-ifs and unfinished plans.

In my hometown in St. Charles Parish, not a soul had forgotten. Not a single person I knew failed to keep his memory alive in some form. Even children hummed the melody of his campaign song, "Every Man a King," which had been written for him by LSU's band director, Castro Carazo. You'd hear it from open windows, being whistled down the road, or sung quietly while working a field. The lyrics had taken on new meaning. They weren't just about hope anymore. They were about remembrance.

People spoke with longing about roads that were never paved, bridges that never connected, and jobs that were never offered. But they didn't talk with bitterness. They talked with belief. They still held on to the idea that those things would have come true if Huey had lived long. And they believed it—not blindly, but fully—with every ounce of conviction their hard lives had taught them to feel.

"Every Man A King"
(Huey P. Long and Castro Carazo.)
Why weep or slumber America
Land of brave and true
With castles and clothing and food for all
All belongs to you
Ev'ry man a king, ev'ry man a king
For you can be a millionaire
If there's something belonging to others
There's enough for all people to share
When it's sunny June and December too
Or in the winter time or spring
There'll be peace without end
Ev'ry neighbor a friend
And ev'ry man a king….

One of those quiet, grieving Louisiana towns—still mourning not just the loss of Huey Long but the slow, stubborn weight of poverty and distance—could be found with little effort. All you had to do was motor twenty-three miles west of the Crescent City, over the recently completed Huey P. Long Bridge. Once you crossed the great structure, iron, and concrete stretching across the river like a promise half-kept, you would find yourself on the other side of both the city and the century. The only road leading into Ama was the River Road, a two-lane ribbon of dust and heat that doubled as the only road out.

That single stretch of road was more than a route. It was a symbol. It defined our place on the map and in the world. The narrowness of that dusty River Road mirrored the limited influence the rest of the world had on Ama—and the limited influence we had on it. This small town, nestled in the crook of the river's west bank, lived in a kind of pocket, shielded by distance and surrounded by familiarity. With roughly 700 souls calling it home, Ama wasn't a place you stumbled upon. You had to mean to go there. And even then, you might miss it.

This part of Louisiana was known as the German Coast, though few outsiders understood what that really meant. Located just upriver from New Orleans, stretching along both banks of the Mississippi, the region had once been known to the French as the Côte des Allemands. Its history was rooted in a promise—a false one. In the early 1700s, a man named John Law, a farmer turned financier, ran the Company of the Indies, which oversaw French colonial Louisiana. Law painted vivid images of a paradise waiting on the other side of the ocean. He spoke of fertile lands and abundant opportunity, and in doing so, he attracted a desperate population of Germans and Alsace-Lorrainers—people worn down by war, hunger, and the theft of their homeland. Law's dream sounded like salvation.

But that dream, like many sold across sea and time, fell apart upon arrival. When the settlers disembarked in Biloxi, they were greeted not by paradise but by hardship. The land was rough, the heat oppressive, the bugs relentless, and the work unending. Of the six thousand settlers who crossed, only two thousand survived the journey. And those who lived discovered soon enough that Law was a fraud. The paradise he had promised was more swamp than soil, more burden than bounty.

Still, these German and French immigrants endured. They adapted. They learned to work the land and, in time, turned hardship into harvest. They discovered the richness of the soil and the bounty it could yield when handled with knowledge and care. Before long, the residents of the German Coast were producing much of the food New Orleans needed to survive. They earned their place not through privilege but through persistence.

No one today knows exactly where the name "Ama" came from. No palindromist has stepped forward to claim it. No historian has bothered to chase down its origins with any real commitment. There are stories, of course. Folklore whispers that the town was named after the daughter of a man who owned Alice Plantation. Others say the word "Ama" means "to love" in Greek. Maybe it does. Maybe it doesn't. Either way, it's all Greek to me.

What I do know is that God smiled on Ama, or at least spared it enough to make it beautiful in its own quiet way. The landscape is dotted with massive, regal live oaks, trees so large and so old that their moss-covered limbs grow long enough to touch the damp, alluvial soil beneath them. These trees stand like guardians, their limbs reaching out like arms—some twisted, some gentle, some stretching along the ground as if they too were tired of standing.

The land itself is as flat as a debutante's chest, and if not for the oaks and the Spanish moss that hangs from nearly every branch like curtains of lace, there would be little in the way of natural beauty to suggest to a traveler that Ama is worth stopping for, much less settling in. The horizon doesn't rise. It stretches. And on still days, it feels as though the whole town might simply drift off into the river unnoticed.

And it nearly did once.

In 1912, the Mississippi River came for Ama. It breached the levee at a place called the Hymelia Crevasse, and for a time, it looked like the entire town might be erased. The waters rose with fury and purpose, threatening to wipe Ama off the map before it had even found its place there. But somehow, by grace or grit, the town survived. It held its ground, soaked but standing.

The tallest things in Ama are not buildings. They are not church steeples or water towers. They are the levees—those giant, silent walls of earth that run alongside the Mississippi River like sentries, watching. Thirty feet high and a hundred feet wide at the base, they are the only thing standing between the town and disaster. Without them, Ama would have long ago joined the ranks of lost places—Atlantis, Aztlan, El Dorado—talked about but never visited.

But this isn't just true of Ama. Every town from Baton Rouge to the Gulf owes its continued existence to the levees. They hold back more than water. They hold back erasure. With the levees, there is life. There is hope. There is the fragile dream of continuity. Without them, there is only water, rolling in with no intention of leaving.

It's hard to believe that the towering levees we see today—those immense earthen walls stretching from Plaquemines Parish to Baton Rouge—were once nothing more than narrow mounds of dirt piled hastily by settlers who had little more than faith and shovels to protect their land. The original levees built along the Mississippi River were crude and fragile by comparison, standing just two feet high and only six feet wide. They were the first line of defense against a river that rose with rage every spring, during the high water months, threatening to consume everything it bordered.

These early settlers had little choice. Owning land along the Mississippi came with the responsibility of protecting it. If you didn't build a levee shortly after claiming property near the river, you risked not only losing your fields to floodwater but also forfeiting your ownership rights altogether. Over time, these mounds were reinforced, widened, and raised, generation after generation, as floods taught lessons and necessity-bred invention. For more than two centuries, the people who lived and farmed along the German Coast worked to shore up these barriers, never fully trusting them, always fearing the breaches they called crevasses.

The fear was not unfounded. A crevasse wasn't just an inconvenience. It was devastation. It meant water pouring in like a beast unchained, swallowing crops, homes, and sometimes lives. Each time it happened, the community responded with grit but never without grief. The river was as much a threat as it was a blessing.

Among the few institutions that held steady through these dangers was the Catholic Church. In this small town, it wasn't just the only religion—it was the framework of daily life. The Church's presence extended into every corner of the parish. Its rituals, rules, and rhythms gave order to a place that otherwise existed on the edge of nature's chaos. For most families in Ama, the Church didn't merely suggest how to live; it defined it.

There was a saying that floated around with good humor and surprising truth: "As long as you don't eat meat on Fridays and confess your sins, you can just about get away with anything." We lived by that rhythm. Confession, communion, feast days, fasting—all of it was just part of who we were. The Church didn't just preach religion; it gave people a sense of stability in a region where everything else could change overnight.

But its greatest gift was constancy. In a place where floods could erase neighborhoods and where economic hardship visited more often than prosperity, the Church was always there. The church bell rang whether the crops were good or failed. It rang for weddings and funerals. And in those days when people didn't have much, they still had their faith. It bound us together. It steadied us when the ground itself felt like it might give way.

As children growing up near the banks of the Mississippi, we found our own kind of constancy in the batture—that narrow strip of land between the levee and the river's edge. To us, it was a wonderland. It was our playground, our secret base, our training ground. I couldn't tell you when I learned to swim or who first taught me. It seemed like I was born knowing. We were always in the water, and the river was always there.

Our parents forbade it, of course. Swimming in the Mississippi was strictly off-limits. There were safer places—bayous, canals, backwater channels that posed far less risk. But safety never had much appeal to a group of teenage boys convinced of their own invincibility. We were told from the time we could understand words that the Mississippi was not for play. We were to fish from its banks, not dive from them.

But warnings had a way of fading beneath the thrill of the forbidden. The river called to us. It offered something the bayous never could. It offered danger—real danger—and that was its allure. Its muddy waters flowed fast and deep, hiding currents that could rip a grown man from his footing in seconds. The river bent and turned without mercy, carving out whirlpools and drop-offs where footing vanished, and the world tilted sideways.

And it wasn't just the natural threats we ignored. The Mississippi was littered with hazards. Beneath that brown surface lay sunken branches, uprooted trees, wreckage from old barges, ropes, nets, broken crates, and all manner of debris tossed into the current from ports and vessels upstream. There were trotlines hidden below the surface, anchored with weights, waiting to hook fish—or an unsuspecting limb. It was a cluttered graveyard of lost cargo and forgotten equipment, and we swam through it like it was a clean, calm lake.

The river was filled with snags, and we knew it. We just chose to ignore it. We thought we could outswim the risk. We thought our youth made us immune. But the real terrors were the ones we couldn't see or even imagine. The Mississippi held secrets under its shifting surface—whirlpools, eddies, and undertows caused by sandbars, rock shifts, or even tree trunks lodged on the bottom. These currents could pull a person under and hold them there with a strength that felt almost human.

You didn't fight the Mississippi. You didn't challenge it, not if you wanted to live.

But in 1937, a new threat had entered the river—one that didn't churn or pull or crush but poisoned instead. As industrialization began creeping up and down the river from New Orleans to Baton Rouge, petroleum plants and small chemical facilities had begun to pop up along the water's edge. They came for the same reason we did—access to the river. It offered cheap labor, easy disposal, and a direct link to the Gulf and beyond.

But their presence carried a price. Waste was dumped freely, often directly into the water, no matter how toxic. Ballast water from ships carried foreign contaminants. Runoff from factories mingled with fish and swimmers alike. The very river we depended on to feed us and carry our goods was also now burning skin, stinging eyes, and possibly doing harm we couldn't yet see.

Still, we loved the river. It gave more than it took—until it didn't. It was our highway, our pantry, our backyard, and our escape. It gave us the fertile soil that fed our crops. It gave us fish, transport, and even recreation. But like any powerful thing, it demanded respect. If you ignored it, if you provoked it, it could take everything. You didn't poke the eye of the tiger.

Too many people in our community had learned that the hard way. Stories floated among us like driftwood—stories of men pulled under, and boys lost to the current, families torn apart in seconds. And yet, every time we stood at the levee and looked out over the water, we felt the same pull.

Because for all its danger, the river gave us something more important than food or work. It gave us a kind of permanence. It was always there. It moved, yes, and it changed, but it never disappeared. We could count on its presence, even if we feared what lay beneath it.

As Tennyson once wrote, "For men may come and men may go, but I go on forever." For those of us in Ama, that wasn't poetry. That was the Mississippi River.

CHAPTER 2

PROVIDENCE PLANTATION

In Ama, commerce didn't hum with variety or flourish with options. It moved at the pace of one place and one man—Providence Plantation, owned and operated by a figure as larger-than-life as the land he commanded: Thomas Joshua Sanders. In this quiet community nestled against the Mississippi, Providence was the only enterprise of any real consequence. And Sanders, by ambition, determination, and perhaps a touch of river-worn luck, had made himself a local legend.

His story, like so many born of the river, began humbly. Sanders started as a mud clerk—one of those lowly errand boys who spent their days hauling, cleaning, and fetching on steamboats, soaking up the culture of the river even as the mud-soaked through their boots. But Sanders didn't stay at the bottom for long. Over time, through grit and cunning, he rose through the ranks and eventually owned the very vessel he once labored on. That arc—from errand boy to riverboat owner—earned him more than a modest fortune. It earned him a reputation.

Local lore passed around without much concern for evidence claimed that Sanders once met Samuel Clemens—the great Mark Twain himself. Some say they became lifelong friends, bound by a shared appreciation for river stories and southern eccentricities. The family, to their credit, admits there's no proof of such a friendship.

But the rumor persists because around here, a man's myth is often more important than his biography.

To the people of Ama, the legacy of Thomas Joshua Sanders wasn't measured by books or politics. It was measured by earth and water. And by that standard, he had built his own monument—Sanders's Canal. Now, the Egyptians built the Pyramids, the Chinese built the Great Wall, and Sanders built a twenty-mile canal through the heart of South Louisiana. Of course, only one of those wonders ran through Ama, and while its impact might not have been global, its ambition was impressive in its own right.

Sanders's Canal was dug from Providence Plantation, winding its muddy way through Lakes Cataouatche and Salvador, all the way to Grand Isle on the Gulf Coast. The idea, as grand as any, was to give his family a watery shortcut to their vacation cottage and, perhaps more importantly, a reliable escape route when hurricane season came calling. Hurricanes didn't make appointments. They arrived with wind and fury. And Sanders wanted a way out that didn't rely on roads or bridges. Whether the canal fulfilled that purpose was up for debate, but it certainly made a statement.

Today, Sanders's Canal still bears his name, though its use has dwindled. Now, it serves more duck hunters than hurricane evacuees. Occasionally, a hunter will steer his pirogue, a shallow draft flatboat through its waters, chasing early morning flights of mallards. More frequently, it plays host to nutria—those massive, rat-like rodents that paddle silently through the wetlands in search of roots, rhizomes, and tender marsh plants. Nutria, not native to Louisiana, were brought over by fur traders from South America some years back and quickly made themselves at home. They joined mink and muskrat in the trapping industry, but unlike those animals, the nutria multiplied at a rate that the ecosystem—and locals—struggled to keep up with.

Even so, Sanders's Canal remains. It may not have become the grand passage its builder envisioned, but it stands as a testament to the man's imagination and energy. If not to his judgment, then at least to his relentless initiative. In a place where so many built nothing, Sanders had carved his mark into the land and left it there, flowing quietly under the Louisiana sun.

The economy of Ama wasn't complicated. It rested on three pillars—Providence Plantation, God, and the rain He provided. The first gave us work. The second gave us hope. The third determined whether we'd have food on the table. Cotton, people liked to say, was king in the South. But here, sugar cane was queen. And in truth, the river parishes were made for sugar. The land, the humidity, the cycle of flooding and receding—it all worked together like a seasonal machine.

Sugar cane wasn't new to Louisiana. Long before Ama had levees or Sanders had canals, Iberville, the founder of the territory, had grown sugar in these parts. But the plant didn't become a crop of real consequence until the Jesuit missionaries got involved. They carried cuttings and plants back from their travels in the Caribbean and began planting them in the fields that now lie beneath sprawling cities like New Orleans. The Church didn't just shape the souls of Louisiana—it shaped its agriculture, too.

Mr. Sanders, who loved a good origin story as much as anyone, often shared one in particular with pride. He'd tell how the sugar cane industry truly took off when a man named Etienne de Boré, who had married the daughter of a local woman, developed the first method for granulating sugar. This happened just a few miles upriver in Destrehan and changed the entire sugar economy. Before that, sugar was a sticky, raw mess. Afterward, it was a refined, profitable product. And once it could be processed and stored more easily, demand exploded.

But the real turning point came with the arrival of steam power. Just as it had transformed the world of shipping, steam power revolutionized sugar production. It replaced the slow muscle of horses and mules with roaring engines and spinning gears. Crude presses gave way to mills. Manual hauling was replaced by mechanical conveyance. And in that transformation, a bond was forged between three men: Mr. Sanders, my grandfather, and eventually, my father.

Steam made sugar big business. And it was in the roar of those early engines, deep in the mills of Providence Plantation, where that bond first took shape.

Just as the people of Ama depended on Providence Plantation, God, and the unpredictable mercy of rain, so too did Mr. Thomas Joshua Sanders have his own trifecta of reliance. His plantation ran on three pillars: cheap labor, machines that never slept, and a man named Paul Manz—first the son of Sidney Toussaint Manz and, eventually, my father.

While others saw machines as cold tools or expensive assets, Mr. Sanders saw them as the muscle behind his sugar empire. But machines don't run themselves. They break. They groan. They require a kind of attention that borders on affection. That's where my father came in. Mr. Sanders may have owned the steel, but my father gave it breath. And if something on the plantation turned, whirred, or burned fuel, it was only because my daddy had made it so.

Paul Manz was born in 1900, a new-century child, into the sturdy hands and work-worn values of Sidney Toussaint Manz. From his father, he inherited two things: an unshakable love for anything mechanical and a face that could not, by any generous standard, be called handsome. He came from solid German stock—broad, tough, quiet. His hair was thick and coal black, a full crown that no comb could tame. His forehead, on the other hand, was almost nonexistent, barely clearing his eyebrows, which may have been the reason God—or genetics—decided to economize by giving him just one long, uninterrupted brow that stretched across both eyes like a firm warning.

But it was his nose that dominated his features, long and wide and unavoidable. It gave his already narrow face a kind of unintentional intensity. He was a tall man—six feet two inches—built like he could lift oxen if he had to. Broad shoulders, massive arms, hands that could crush but rarely needed to. My father wasn't the kind of man who sought fights, but anyone foolish enough to start one with him learned quickly that they had misjudged the odds.

Whatever he may have lacked in traditional appearance, the Lord repaid him with character—and in abundance. My father was smart, not in the way schools tend to reward but in the way the world respects. His formal education ended the same day his father's life did. My grandfather died in a tragic accident at Providence Plantation, though to this day, no one in our parish ever seemed willing to describe to me exactly what happened. They'd talk endlessly about who he was, what he meant, and how deeply he was admired. But when it came to his death, there was only silence. The kind of silence that's too heavy to lift.

I was still a boy when I began hearing stories about my grandfather. They came from neighbors, from older men in town, from widows who remembered the way he used to tip his hat. It didn't matter where I was—in the church hall, at the store, or near the levee—his name was spoken with respect. Yet, never once did anyone describe the moment he was taken. That, I suppose, was their way of preserving his dignity. Or perhaps it was too painful a scene to retell.

On the day of his death, my father was just 14 years old. A boy, really. But from that moment forward, he became the man of the house. He stepped into a role far too large for his age but somehow made it fit. Overnight, he went from apprentice to cornerstone—of both home and plantation. Mr. Sanders didn't hesitate. He entrusted my father with keeping the machinery of Providence running. And my father rose to meet that trust the way he approached everything in life—with quiet resolve.

My dad didn't learn machines. He understood them the way some men understand animals or music. He could hear a faulty belt from across the field. He could touch a boiler and tell you what was wrong with it. There was no blueprint for what he did. No manual. Just a natural instinct and relentless hands.

When I was old enough to lift a wrench without dragging it, I became his shadow. I followed him into barns, under tractors, into the belly of rumbling mills. Summer breaks, weekends, holidays—we didn't take time off. My time with him was in the grease and the grind. Shoulder to shoulder, elbow-deep in fuel and steam. I watched the way he worked: efficient, focused, never rushed, but never slow. I paid attention to the way he spoke to the machines—as if they were living things, as if they listened.

He loved the work. That's what struck me most. My father didn't repair machines out of duty. He did it out of affection, out of pride. He respected their purpose, their strength, and the people they served. And through that, I came to love the work too—not just for the satisfaction of fixing something, but because it meant I was near him.

As time went on, word of his skill spread beyond Ama. He wasn't just fixing engines and grinders at Providence anymore. His hands kept machines running from Ama to Donaldsonville and likely farther than that. But he didn't stop at repairs. My father started improving things. He reimagined equipment, added pulleys, adjusted gear ratios, and repurposed steam flow. He wasn't content to maintain; he wanted to innovate.

With nothing but an idea, a box of tools, a drive belt, and some scrap parts, he could build mechanisms that saved hours of labor and made sugar production smoother, faster, and more profitable. All of this, mind you, before he turned thirty. By then, many plantation owners along the German Coast knew his name, and more importantly, they knew his value. They wanted him. They offered money, tools, and positions. But time was the one thing he never had enough of.

And no matter how far his reputation spread, my father never left Mr. Sanders behind. He remembered the man who gave him his first job, who trusted a 14-year-old boy with the lifeblood of a plantation. My father never forgot that. Loyalty wasn't a choice for him—it was a principle. He helped others when he could, but Providence always came first.

Mr. Sanders might have owned the plantation. But as far as the machinery was concerned, it was my father who kept the heart beating.

Almost all the men my father worked alongside at Providence Plantation were cut from the same cloth. Their roots reached back to Germany or the Alsace-Lorraine region of France, and their families had come to Louisiana generations earlier, often with little more than determination and a name hard to pronounce. They were men who knew hard work and didn't expect anyone else to carry their burdens for them. They spoke with quiet voices, rough hands, and the kind of loyalty that didn't need to be said out loud.

But there were exceptions. Not many—but a few. Among them was John Washington Robert, a man everyone called J.W., though no one ever seemed to agree on whether it stood for anything more than his name. J.W. was, by every measure, a fixture at Providence. He had been working there since before my father had even been born. As he used to say with a wink, he'd been employed there "since I was old enough to walk the mile and a half from Mama's porch to Mr. Sanders's barn."

One day, I asked him, plain as a child can, "Mr. J.W., have you worked here your whole life?"

He didn't pause. Didn't think. Just smiled that wide, weathered grin and replied, "Not yet."

It was the kind of answer that said everything and nothing at once. That was J.W.

According to my dad—and I say this knowing his bias—J.W. was the second-best mechanic he'd ever known. The best, of course, being my grandfather. But even that was a close call. J.W. had worked side by side with my grandfather before the accident that changed everything. After that terrible day, when my father was thrust into the role of provider at just 14, it was J.W. who stepped in quietly. He didn't announce it. He didn't ask permission. He just took my father under his wing and kept teaching him everything he knew about machines, tools, steam pressure, gear teeth, and patience. In many ways, J.W. became the father figure my dad had lost, and my father, in turn, loved him for it, not with words, but with loyalty.

J.W. was not a large man by height. He was compact—short, thick in the chest and arms, solid like someone carved from a block of wood that refused to split. But he had a strength that defied logic. I saw him lift an engine block once, straight off the ground, with nothing but a grunt and a grip that could turn steel. If a bolt was rusted beyond reason and wouldn't budge, J.W. never hesitated. He'd grab a length of pipe, slide it over the wrench handle, and, with the added leverage, break that bolt loose like it was nothing. He never let the machine win.

His face was unforgettable .....dark, black and parched by too many days working in the humidity and heat of Louisiana summers. A full, wiry gray beard curled wildly around his chin as if trying to keep up with his energy. His eyebrows were just as rebellious, thick, and unkempt, perched over eyes that missed nothing. His hair—what was left of it—was bushy, wild, and thinned at the top. It looked as though it had been at war with a hat for most of its life and had only barely survived.

J.W. had lost most of his teeth long ago, though it never seemed to bother him. When he spoke, his top lip all but disappeared, and when he ate, his nose bobbed with every chew, a rhythm that made people smile without even realizing it. His nostrils flared wide, his lips full and expressive. Even his thick mustache couldn't hide the permanent grin that seemed etched into his face. Everyone loved J.W., not because he asked for it but because he earned it. And because you just couldn't help it.

One of the most important lessons my father ever taught me didn't come from a sermon or a speech. It came from how he treated men like J.W. My dad didn't speak about equality. He lived it. He never drew a line between himself and the colored men he worked with. He respected ability, effort, and loyalty. Skin color didn't mean a thing to him—not in the shop, not in the field, not anywhere. As he told me once, "When you're covered in grease and mud, son, everybody looks the same."

He worked with J.W. like a brother. They laughed together, ate lunch under the same tool shed roof, and leaned on each other when the summer heat was thick enough to bend nails. J.W. was the funniest man my father had ever known, and he wasn't afraid to laugh at himself. In fact, those were the moments that made him laugh the hardest. He found joy in his own mistakes, and that humility made him even more beloved.

The summers in South Louisiana were brutal. The heat didn't just sit on your skin—it pressed into your bones. And still, the work never stopped. For two men covered in oil and engine soot, their laughter might've been the only breeze some days. It must've been a kind of gift for both of them to have that bond.

Life in Ama wasn't grand. But it was grounded. We didn't have much, but what we had, we knew how to value. Our home sat less than a mile from Providence Plantation, and like most homes along the River Road between Ama and Vacherie, it was humble, functional, and full of stories. We said we owned it. But truthfully, it was my grandfather's house, passed down more by necessity than inheritance.

When my grandfather died, my father inherited not only the grief but also the responsibility. At 14, he didn't just take over the repairs at the plantation—he took over the house. My grandmother never recovered from her husband's death. Her spirit broke in quiet, permanent ways. She couldn't work, couldn't cook, couldn't care for herself the way she had once done with strength and precision. So my father, still a boy in years, became the caretaker of the home and the heart within it.

The house itself was a classic Cajun cottage, built with function and storms in mind. It had a white cedar board exterior, weathered by time and climate. Its roof was steep—steep enough to shed the near-daily torrential showers that rolled in from the Gulf. The rain didn't trickle off our roof; it cascaded, slapping down like a drumline. I used to lie awake some nights listening to it, the sound rising and falling like a war chant.

The porch was lifted off the ground, standing on blocks to guard against the floods that came every spring. Five steps led to the front door, wide and solid, made of thick cypress. On either side, weather-beaten storm shutters clung faithfully to their hinges—not decorative, but necessary. Around here, hurricanes weren't "if" but "when." Those shutters had faced more than their share of wind.

Four small 2x4 windows flanked the front door like narrow eyes watching the road. Above them, a rusty tin roof stretched across the structure, groaning in the heat and clanging with the rain. When those southern storms came crashing down, our roof sang back in thunderous reply. It was a noisy, chaotic, beautiful sound—the music of home in Ama.

Our house, like many in Ama, was raised about three feet off the ground, resting on blocks. This wasn't some architectural flair. It was a practical necessity. In South Louisiana, flooding was as regular as sunrise. Torrential rains, summer storms, and the occasional hurricane came with such frequency that it wasn't a question of *if* the water would rise—but *when*. That little bit of elevation could mean the difference between a ruined floor and a dry night's sleep.

The front porch ran the full width of the house and was our gathering place, especially in the evenings or on weekends. We spent a lot of time there—rocking in chairs, listening to the cicadas hum, or just watching the wind move the moss in the trees. We called it "B.E."—before electricity. Back then, the porch wasn't just for sitting. It was our entertainment center, our cooling station, and often, our living room.

Inside, the heart of our home was the kitchen. It was large—not elegant, not modern, but filled with life. Grandmother Manz and Mom practically lived in that room. They spent hours every day there, preparing meals with a kind of rhythm and care that today's kitchens rarely see. Our kitchen wasn't built to impress anyone. It was built to work. Function mattered more than form.

At some point, Dad had bought a gas stove, which felt like a marvel compared to the old wood-burning one we had used for as long as I could remember. Still, the ice box remained—a wooden, metal-lined beast that demanded daily attention and a steady supply of ice. Against one wall stood a deep Belfast sink, nearly four feet wide, capable of holding massive pots, kettles, and the aftermath of family meals. In the middle of the room was a round table, oversized and worn smooth from years of elbows, laughter, prayer, and food. It was where everything happened—meals, homework, family meetings, and occasional arguments that fizzled as quickly as they flared.

The kitchen windows were massive and swung open wide, letting in shafts of golden light during the day and, in summer, whatever breeze the Louisiana heat allowed. They served one purpose in winter—light. But in summer, they were our lifeline. They vented out the swelter that built up from cooking and from simply existing in the kind of humid heat that made breathing feel like work.

Our living room had the same no-nonsense spirit. A square room with 12-foot ceilings, it was designed with one goal in mind—comfort during Southern summers. The tall ceilings were more than just architecture. They allowed the rising heat to lift away from where we sat. Double-hung windows surrounded the room, carefully placed to create natural airflow. The bottom sash pulled in cool air while the top released the hot. It was an elegant bit of frontier engineering, and it worked better than you'd think.

In that room, certain chairs had permanent owners. Grandmother's chair, made of heavy wood with worn cushions, was more throne than seat. Its most remarkable feature was a small round button built into one armrest. Press it, and a footrest would pop out while the back reclined—a true marvel for the time. She spent hours there, crocheting doilies that adorned every armrest and table in the house. Her handiwork wasn't just decorative. It sold. Homemakers from all over the German Coast—and even in New Orleans—came asking for her work. She kept us fed not just with cooking but with her craft.

Beside her chair stood a small table that still held Grandfather's pipes and tobacco, untouched since the day he died. It was as if she couldn't bring herself to move them, and maybe she didn't need to. They were a kind of memory that didn't need words.

Across the room sat another large chair—Dad's by default. It was where he settled in at the end of a long day, listening to the evening radio broadcast with a Falstaff in hand, letting the music or the news wash over him as the hum of the house carried on.

Mom's spot was the sofa, a cushioned stretch that took up nearly an entire wall. It was where she escaped into her own rhythm—writing letters, sometimes by candlelight, to relatives in New Orleans or distant cousins still in Molsheim, near Strasbourg, back in the Alsace-Lorraine region of France. She wrote with a kind of joy that made it clear: this was her way of staying connected to the world beyond Ama. I once promised myself that I'd go there one day—see the Rhine, walk the streets of Molsheim, and understand the part of me that had never set foot in Louisiana.

In the middle of that living room, on a circular rug, was my spot. It's where I lay on my stomach and listened to the radio—sports, game shows, news from places I'd never seen. The hardwood floors beneath me were spotless. You could eat off them. And I don't just mean that as a phrase. Grandmother kept that house immaculate. She was always cleaning, sweeping, polishing, or cooking. Her pride in our home was quiet but fierce. She had lost a husband and a future but not her sense of duty.

My little brother Timmy and I shared the upstairs. We reached our room by climbing the stairs from the front porch, a setup that made it feel like a hideaway. The room itself was as big as the entire ground floor. It was open, unfinished, and echoing with our laughter. We'd roughhouse up there until Dad had to reinforce the floorboards—Timmy had nearly fallen through one day after a particularly wild tumble. It wasn't fancy. It wasn't even warm in winter. But it was dry, safe, and ours.

Out back, stood a giant cistern fed by the gutters that wrapped around the roof like a metal halo. Made of thick cypress staves, the cistern collected rainwater, which we used for drinking, cooking, and everything else. Nearly every home in Ama had one. There was no city water to speak of. The sky gave it, and we made do.

Electricity didn't come to Ama all at once. It crept in, carried down lines that followed the River Road like veins. In New Orleans, electricity had arrived decades earlier—in the 1880s. Theaters, hotels, and department stores rushed to electrify, eager for that modern advantage. The Southwest Brush Electric Light and Power Company led the charge, followed by the Edison Electric Illuminating Company. But out here, in the parishes and bayous, it took time.

We were lucky. Because we lived alongside the River Road and its proximity to the west bank's main electric line, we got it sooner than most. And once we had it, everything changed. Bedtime, once dictated by the setting sun, was no longer tied to the candle's final flicker. Now we had light. We had access.

But even more important than the bulb was the radio. It connected us. It brought in the voice of New Orleans, the hum of the outside world, and stories that made us feel like we were part of something larger. Sitting around the radio became a ritual. We'd lean in close, eyes wide, listening to reports, songs, and plays from places we'd never been.

It was radio that introduced us to WWL, a station born from the vision of Jesuit priests at Loyola University in New Orleans. In the early 1930s, these priests had the radical idea to build a radio station—not just for education but to serve the community. Before they could turn that idea into soundwaves, they had to get permission from the top—the Holy See himself. That's right—the Pope approved the station.

When WWL finally broadcast, it did so with 50,000 watts of power, cutting across the Louisiana air like a lightning bolt. It reached all the way into Ama and into homes like ours. We were one of the few families in 1937 to own a radio, and that meant our porch was never empty. Friends, neighbors, and relatives would gather outside, drawn by the glowing sound from inside. The windows would be open, the radio crackling and our front porch would come alive with people hungry to listen.

It wasn't just entertainment. It was connection. And for a small house in a small town along the Mississippi River, that meant everything.

CHAPTER 3

AT HOME

The only thing my dad loved more than working on machinery was my mom, Marie Peyroux Manz. He never had to say it though he never hesitated expressing his love and devotion for her. You could see it in the way he looked at her across the dinner table or how his voice softened just a little when he said her name. They were married in June of 1922, just days after Mom graduated from Hahnville High School. I came along nine months after.

Dad's last day of "formal' education was the same day as his father's death. He would never spend a day at Hahnville High School learning, discovering, and interacting with his friends. As all of his friends gathered to go to school, he went to the plantation to work 8 to 10 hours. His education most assuredly continued at Providence Plantation, granted a much different and, in most respects, a more difficult education as he carried the weight of a man twice his age. The lessons he learned at Providence Plantation, almost all the time, at the side of J. W. Robert, had little to do with biology or history, and the math he learned had more to do with timing on an engine than that of solving equations.

My dad was a good athlete, loved baseball, and was on his way to becoming something special on the baseball diamond. When he wasn't on the batture with his three closest friends, T.J. Breaux, E.J. Talbot, and Keeter St. Amant, he was on the baseball diamond with them playing the game he loved and one in which he flourished. His dreams of pitching in the majors....yes, becoming the next Bill Doak.... for his beloved St. Louis Cardinals was erased in one hot, tragic second at Providence Plantation. But these were the life's lessons he had to learn, as so much and so many depended upon him and the work that he did for Mr. Sanders. But still, it must have been brutal to know that circumstances he had no control over had forced his hand, determined his future for him, and had taken most of his options off the table.

I have often wondered what those years must have been like for my dad as his friends all attended school together and participated in all the extracurricular activities that go along with the high school experience...... a scenario in which he would have excelled. Being unable to participate in these activities had to have been difficult, but he accepted his fate and, at least, to my knowledge, never complained about all these experiences that his friends enjoyed and that he missed.

Paul and Marie Peyroux Manz

The Great War had just ended, and supreme confidence and enthusiasm for the present and the future rippled through the country as opportunities that just a few years ago seemed to be unlikely, now seemed more than probable. But Dad knew those dreams of the future, for him at least, would never extend farther than Ama and Providence Plantation.

Mom often said that she first saw Dad when he was on the pitcher's mound for the Luling Aces baseball team. She said he looked ten feet tall, and no one knows if it was his long frame or the mound that offered that effect, but it really didn't matter as their life together began in a most unlikely place…a baseball diamond. The fact that Dad did not make it past the eighth grade did nothing to discourage Mom from pursuing their relationship. If hard work was the ultimate measure of a man, she knew… and Mom's parents knew... my dad measured up in spades.

The one advantage that my dad had over his friends was that he was the proud owner of his father's Ford pickup and, as the owner, had mobility that most of his friends could only wish for. Barely able to see over the dashboard, the truck offered him the opportunity to spend what little free time he had with his friends and, particularly, with my mom as their friendship blossomed from romance and, eventually, marriage. Sheriff Vicknair, the sheriff of St. Charles Parish, would have certainly arrested any other 14-year-old driving on "his roads," but Dad had a free pass as long as he obeyed the law, stayed out of trouble, and was responsible.

Mom was a wonderful homemaker. She returned my father's adoration without hesitation, as naturally as drawing breath. Her world revolved around him—not in the way of someone who had no life of her own, but in the way of someone who had found where her joy lived. She was happiest at his side, and you could tell. Where Dad stood tall at six-foot-two, broad-shouldered and rugged from long days at the mill and in the fields, Mom was small, delicate in frame, but never in spirit. Her size never seemed to matter much. She carried herself with a kind of quiet strength that made her seem ten feet tall when she needed to be. Her capacity for love was boundless, and zest for life…contagious. You never felt like you were getting what was left over—she gave her best without ever making a show of it, and I adored my mom because of it. If there was one word I'd use to describe my mother, it would be effervescent. That word may not come up often in the parishes of South Louisiana, but it fits her all the same. She had a smile that seemed to be stitched right into her face that was contagious.

She wasn't loud or boisterous, but she moved through life with a kind of lightness that lifted the rest of us. She loved life. She loved people. And when troubles came, as they always do, she refused to let them settle in. She'd square her shoulders, maybe hum a little tune under her breath, and carry on like she'd already figured out how to get past it. Nothing seemed to rattle her. No tragedy, no setback, no stretch of lean times ever shook her footing. She had this steady calm, like the river in early morning—moving, quiet, always there. Her compassion for others was something people remembered. Folks around Ama, and even farther out, spoke of her the same way they spoke of someone who had done them a favor they could never repay. Not because she wanted recognition, but because she always seemed to know what someone needed—and if she could give it, she did.

My grandmother spoke three languages—fluent German, fluent French, and broken English—but none of them captured what she meant to say quite as well as the meals she put on the table. Words were something she managed. Cooking was something she mastered. When I was young, she prepared all our meals. Morning, noon, and night, it was Grandmother at the stove, sleeves rolled up, moving about the kitchen like she was born there. And what a cook she was.

There wasn't a dish she couldn't handle, and there wasn't a guest who left our home hungry. She didn't use recipes or measure much of anything. She cooked by feel and by memory. Her hands moved with the confidence of someone who had made the same meals hundreds of times, and yet every dish came out like it was her best one. But time, as it does, wore her down. Her knees didn't bend the way they used to. Her hands, once so quick and sure, had started to tremble. She held onto her apron for longer than most expected, and eventually, she had to hand over cooking duties to my mother. That transition wasn't easy for her. She didn't say much about it, but I could tell it meant something. Still, she stepped aside without complaint and let Mom take the reins. And though Mom did a fine job—and I mean that—there was something about Grandmother's cooking that never quite left us. When she could cook, she cooked like it mattered.

We ate a lot of seafood in those days. Shrimp, oysters, crabs—all of it local, all of it fresh, all of it delicious. Seafood was never hard to come by, especially for families living along the River Road. But in our house, we never ate fish. Not ever. Not once. Not fried, nor baked, and courtbillion and bouillabaisse, both a kind of fish stew or soup and popular around here, were totally out of the question. Fish, in all its forms, was banned from the house by my mother. She couldn't stand the smell of it. She said it stayed in the curtains and clung to our clothes. She didn't want it in her kitchen, and certainly didn't want it in the ice box, and made it very clear that if you went fishing, you'd best figure out what to do with the catch before you stepped back inside her house.

And we did go fishing. Often. Dad and I would take our cane poles and walk down to the batture, maybe toss a line into a quiet bayou or, more likely, in the river itself. We caught a lot, too—catfish, bream, perch—but those fish never crossed the threshold of our house.

Because of that, I never developed a taste for it. Not even curiosity. If it wasn't allowed in the house, it wasn't part of life. Even now, all these years later, I won't eat fish. It's not that I dislike it. It's that I never learned to want it.

Grandmother's cooking, though, was a different story altogether. She made the kinds of meals that seemed to have a memory built into them. There were the usual South Louisiana favorites—shrimp creole, rich and red, though every now and then she forgot to add the shrimp. We didn't complain. There was gumbo, thick and dark, and étouffées that steamed on the plate like something pulled out of a dream. She made sauce piquant so spicy you had to sit still for a moment after the first bite, just to catch your breath. And every Monday, without fail, was wash day, and that meant red beans and rice with a giant ham hock right in the center. It was the kind of meal that felt earned. My dad and I would playfully squabble over who got the ham bone. It was a tradition as dependable as the meal itself.

But Grandmother didn't just cook the typical dishes you'd expect to find in South Louisiana. She brought flavors to our table that none of my friends' mothers dared try. Her kitchen smelled different, richer, and more complicated. You could walk in the door and know within seconds that she wasn't making the same thing you'd find in every other home along the road. There were hints of the Old World, little touches she carried with her from the Alsace-Lorraine tradition, folded quietly into our Louisiana life. Her meals told a story. And in our family, those meals stayed with us longer than most conversations ever could.

I think part of the reason our home, and especially our kitchen, carried such a distinct flavor—both literally and otherwise—came down to our French and German heritage. That mix of backgrounds wasn't just something we talked about at reunions. It lived in the food, the language, the music, the way we spoke, and even how we greeted people at the door. It was stitched into everything we did, whether we noticed it or not. My great-grandmother arrived in Louisiana around 1850, part of a small group of settlers from the German-speaking regions of Alsace-Lorraine. They had left behind everything they knew, chasing the promise of a better life. The journey took them across the Atlantic, landing in Biloxi, then the port of New Orleans, and then by boat up the great river until they reached St. Charles Parish, roughly thirty miles upriver, on the west bank. That's where they settled, in a stretch of land that would, for years, be known by the French as les Allemands—the Germans.

That little name, whispered in accents from both sides of the Rhine, would become part of our identity. Over time, the entire stretch became commonly referred to as the German Coast, and it remained a quiet hub of settlement for others who came after. The land was rich, the river close, and the sense of community strong enough to carry people through the hardest seasons. You didn't need much if you had your family, your neighbors, and something growing in the ground.

The Germans who came—people like my great-grandmother—arrived speaking two languages but those who arrived speaking only German, quickly found themselves needing another. They started learning French almost immediately, out of necessity more than curiosity. Marriages with the early French settlers followed soon after, and in time, those blended families became part of the fabric of the region. It wasn't long before they were also marrying into Cajun families, which only further blurred the cultural lines. Language, food, music—it all mixed together in a way that felt natural, like branches growing into each other. You could see the French influence most clearly in the names. Over time, German names were reshaped to fit the French tongue. It wasn't always formal, and it wasn't forced, but it happened just the same. Zehringer became Zeringue. Heidel turned into Haydel. Himmel became Hymel, Rommel into Rome, and Trischl smoothed into Triche. That sort of change was common, expected even. Most families didn't think twice about it.

But ours didn't follow the pattern. Where others adapted, we held on. Most of the families around Ama and the nearby parishes saw Manz shift into Montz, softening with time and usage. But not us. It was my grandfather who put his foot down. He never said much about why, but I think he saw the name as something worth keeping as it was. It wasn't about pride so much as a quiet kind of insistence.

That was his name, and he wasn't interested in seeing it turned into something easier for others to pronounce.

There wasn't bitterness in his decision—just resolve. He knew where we came from, and he saw no need to smooth the edges off something that already fit just fine. So while names changed all around us, ours stayed the same. We remained Manz. That stubbornness, or steadiness depending on how you saw it, seemed to run in the family. And looking back, I'm glad it did. Because my grandmother was originally from the Alsace-Lorraine region, her cooking followed the traditions she had grown up with, the same ones passed down to her by her mother. It wasn't something she talked about much. She didn't explain where each recipe came from or which generation had first stirred the pot. She just cooked the way she had always known, and the results spoke for themselves.

We ate meals that most families in Ama had never heard of. Dishes with names that didn't roll off the tongue for anyone who hadn't grown up hearing them. And while rice was the staple starch on just about every table up and down the River Road, at our house, it was potatoes. We had them in some form or another with nearly every meal. Mashed, boiled, fried in a pan with onions, tucked into casseroles, or folded into dough. It wasn't even a question. If there was a plate, there was a potato.

Of course, we still took full advantage of the seafood Louisiana had to offer—shrimp, crab, oysters. As long as it didn't swim like a fish, Mom was fine with it. But alongside that coastal fare, Grandmother served up meals that belonged to a colder climate, meals full of vinegar, root vegetables, and rich, hearty sauces. I have often thought that two women of such diverse backgrounds in one kitchen was asking for trouble and was a recipe for disaster. But it speaks volumes for the kind of women they both were as they shared one thing in the kitchen that brought them together, and that was the fact that they were preparing food for Dad, Timmy, and me…three people they loved more than life itself.

There was pork knuckle with sauerkraut, the kind of dish that simmered all afternoon and filled the house with a sharp, warm smell that somehow made you hungry and cautious at the same time. There was hoppel poppel, which was something like an omelet, but tossed together with potatoes and sausage and whatever vegetables were lying around. She made Sauerbraten, marinated and slow-cooked until it was almost too tender to slice, and Wiener Schnitzel, which my friends just called paneed meat, breaded and fried and always gone in seconds. There was chicken with Knödel, the German version of chicken and dumplings, with big doughy lumps that soaked up the broth so well you'd almost forget the chicken was there. And there was Spaetzle, too—little hand-rolled noodles dropped into boiling water and fried in butter with onions or cheese.

Then came the sweets. Franz buns, which were something like cinnamon rolls but with a firmer bite. Potato pancakes, thin and crispy on the edges. Apple Cinnamon Kaiserschmarrn, torn pieces of sweet batter cooked like crepes but thicker, dusted with sugar and dotted with fruit. There was Cinnamon Apfelkuchen, soft and tart with slices of apple folded through. She made gingerbread cookies she called Pfeffernüsse, small and spicy and a little crunchy, and there was always apple custard cake cooling on the windowsill whenever there were leftover apples from the neighbor's orchard.

Come the holidays, we'd have mincemeat pie, made with raisins and spices and whatever else she had on hand. Bread pudding showed up on the table regularly, heavy with raisins and cinnamon, and swimming in vanilla so strong you could smell it from outside. And then, of course, there was cheese. Always cheese. Soft, hard, creamy, crumbly. Most of it I liked well enough, but there were a few I avoided with the same commitment I gave to avoiding fish. Grandmother had a brick of Backstein cheese in the ice box at all times—it smelled like Limburger and looked like trouble—and a wedge of blue cheese that no one else in the family would touch but her.

In the fall, as the weather cooled just enough to give us a break from the heat, she'd make homemade Lebkuchen syrup, a gingerbread syrup she kept in a little corked bottle on the shelf. She used it on everything. Pancakes, toast, even her coffee. And on the mornings when her sweet tooth leaned toward the stronger side, she'd take her coffee "sweetened" with schnapps. She never offered it to anyone else and never apologized for it. It was her little indulgence, and nobody questioned it.

Grandmother Manz

We even had andouille sausage and bratwurst, thanks to a local farmer who had recently come over from Germany. He raised hogs just outside of town and made the best sausage in the area. Grandmother swore by him and wouldn't buy meat from anyone else. Both sausages were regulars on our table, often fried up in the same cast iron skillet she'd had since before I was born.

Looking back, it's no wonder the house always smelled like something was cooking. Between the seafood, the stews, the baked goods, and the cheese, our kitchen was a patchwork of two continents—and everything we ate came with a story, even if it wasn't spoken.

Every morning, without fail, Grandmother and Mom baked biscuits. It was as much a part of our morning as the sunrise or the sound of the river shifting in the distance. The kitchen would already be warm by the time Timmy and I stumbled out of bed, the smell of flour and shortening already thick in the air. They baked enough for the family, of course, but they always made about half a dozen more—big, golden-brown biscuits—just for the "visitors."

Our house sat right on the only real road that cut across the west bank of the river. You could argue whether it ran north-south or east-west, depending on how the river bent and how technical you wanted to get. But either way, it was the main line for anyone heading through Ama on foot. With the country still gripped by the Great Depression, we saw a steady trickle of strangers pass by. They came quietly, often alone, carrying nothing but the clothes on their backs and the weight of hard times in their eyes.

Many were sent our way by someone else—a neighbor, a cousin, a church friend—someone who had once needed help themselves and knew that my mother and grandmother would not turn anyone away. These visitors didn't knock. They didn't ask for anything. They didn't have to. They just stood outside the gate at the edge of our yard, still as shadows, staring at the house like it held something holy inside. They never begged. Never pleaded. Most of them looked too proud, or maybe too broken, to do anything more than stand there. Some would nod when we came out to greet them. Some just looked away. They wore ragged clothes, often too big or too small, sleeves torn, pants held up by rope or string. Their feet were usually bare, callused and dirty, as though they walked for days without rest. But what I remember most, even more than the clothes or the silence, was the look in their eyes—a hollow, tired stare that seemed to say the world had stopped being kind a long time ago.

Mom never asked questions. She didn't need to. She always knew why they were there. Without a word, she'd send me or Timmy out to tell them to stay put, that we had something for them—as if they had somewhere else to be. While Grandmother reached for the cane syrup, Mom would work with quiet care. She'd take a spoon and gently make a hole in the side of each biscuit, just deep enough to hold what was coming. Then she'd pour in the syrup—rich, dark, and sweet—until the biscuit was filled to its limit. The cane syrup would soak into the warm bread and spill just slightly down the side, sticky and perfect. Once they were filled, Mom wrapped each one in whatever scrap of paper she had set aside—old newspaper, saved wrapping paper, whatever had been pressed flat and stored in the kitchen drawer for just this purpose. It wasn't elegant, but it was thoughtful, neat, and handed over with a smile.

She'd walk the biscuits out to the gate herself, hand them over one by one like she was giving something far more valuable than food. Sometimes, she'd touch a shoulder or speak a quiet word. Other times, she'd just smile and watch as they nodded and turned to leave, heading off down the road like smoke in the wind. And then, as she made her way back to the porch, she'd look out at the road a little longer than necessary. More than once I heard her murmur something about where their next meal would come from. She never said it to us, not directly, but you could hear the ache in her voice. It bothered her to send them away with so little, even though it was more than most would offer.

My father, for his part, was just as generous—though in a different way. He did a lot of mechanical work for small sugar cane growers and sharecroppers across the parish. Most of them couldn't pay much, and many couldn't pay at all. Still, Dad never turned them down. If he got anything in return, it was usually a jar or can of cane syrup. I used to wonder why we always had so much of it in the pantry. Shelves lined with metal cans and glass jars, sealed and sticky around the edges. It wasn't until later that I understood. All that syrup wasn't for us. It was for the visitors.

HOPPEL POPPEL

(Somewhat like an omelet with potatoes)

INGREDIENTS:

- About 1-pound leftover cooked meat
- 1 - large onions, finely chopped
- 4 tablespoons butter
- 1 pound of leftover boiled potatoes
- Salt, pepper
- 8 eggs

INSTRUCTIONS:

1. Cut the potatoes into thin slice so they will cook faster.
2. Fry the onions in 2 tablespoons butter until tender and add the meat that has been thinly cut into strips.
3. Add remaining 2 tablespoons butter and the potatoes.
4. Continue frying till potatoes are golden brown.
5. Season with salt and pepper.

6. Mix the eggs and pour over the meat and potatoes. Carefully stir until eggs are the way you like them.

Our home

CHAPTER 4

TIME IN THE PRINCIPAL'S OFFICE

My freshman year at Hahnville High School didn't begin with the glory I had imagined. I had pictured a strong, respectable start—a clean slate, new classes, maybe even some kind of recognition for carrying the Manz name. Instead, it kicked off with a dust-up behind the cafeteria and a trip straight to the principal's office. Not exactly the kind of distinction I had in mind, but memorable all the same.

It happened on the very first day of school. I got into it with a classmate who was three years older than me and stood at least a foot taller. I don't remember what exactly sparked it—maybe a glance held too long, but the next thing I knew, fists were flying and I was trying not to end up face-first in the dirt.

He definitely got the better of me. By the time a teacher pulled us apart, my shirt was torn, and I was sporting a decent black eye, busted ribs, a skinned jaw, and a swollen lip.

But I got in a couple of solid licks, and that counted for something. I didn't win the fight, but I walked away knowing I'd at least made a point: I wasn't someone who backed down, no matter the odds. Around Hahnville, that mattered.

But my "situation" at Hahnville High wasn't like anyone else's. It wasn't just different. It was one of a kind. You see, the principal of Hahnville High had done the unthinkable. He'd married my father's sister, Catherine. Which meant the man sitting behind that wide oak desk—the man whose job it was to discipline me, evaluate me, and decide if I belonged in that school—was my uncle.

Mr. Lucien Labry.

Of course, I still called him Mr. Labry, not Uncle Lucien. Calling him anything else felt impossible, not just because he ran the school, but because he terrified me. Respect didn't even begin to cover it. I said, "Mr. Labry," with the same tone a soldier uses when addressing a general.

He looked exactly the way you'd imagine a high school principal should. Always in a suit. Not once, did I ever see him in a sports coat, much less without a jacket altogether. Shirt pressed crisp. Tie straight as a plumb line. The man looked like he'd stepped out of a textbook diagram labeled "Discipline."

He wasn't large in stature, but he didn't need size to intimidate. His presence did all the work. He'd fought in the Great War, and though we never heard him speak of it, people in town still called him "Colonel" out of habit and respect. It suited him.

His hair was thick and dark, combed straight back with some kind of pomade that kept it frozen in place. It always looked wet, slicked down to perfection. Even on the hottest Louisiana afternoons, his hair never moved an inch. It was unsettling in its own right, but what really unnerved people were his eyes.

He wore tiny round glasses, the kind with thin wire frames, and they made his eyes seem larger than life. Those lenses didn't just magnify—they exaggerated, emphasized, and turned every glance into a stare. And he didn't blink like the rest of us. When Mr. Labry looked at you, he didn't just see you. He examined you. Judged you. Convicted you, if needed.

Talking to him felt like being cross-examined. You'd start answering a question and suddenly forget whether you were guilty of something or not. His eyes were too much. It wasn't just the glasses. It was the way he looked through people, like he could see the thoughts forming before you spoke. It didn't matter how innocent you were—you felt guilty under that stare and you never knew if you were talking to him or being analyzed by him.

So there I was, on my very first day as a freshman, shirt torn, black eye, skinned jaw, lip swollen, and busted ribs, sitting in the front office waiting to be summoned into what might as well have been a courtroom. I wasn't just any student. I was the principal's nephew. And if that came with any kind of privilege, I hadn't seen it yet. I braced myself as the door creaked open, and the secretary motioned me in. It was time to face the judge.

Mr. Labry had been an educator his entire life. Teaching wasn't just a job for him—it was a calling, maybe even a mission. After serving his country in the Great War, he returned home and enrolled at Louisiana State University, earning his degree in the early 1920s. He didn't take a break, didn't waste time figuring things out. He went straight into the classroom.

His first post was at a small school in Kenner, Louisiana, where he taught math to kids who likely had no idea they were sitting in front of a man who would one day run the most prominent high school in St. Charles Parish. He taught there for several years—quietly, effectively, with the kind of discipline and precision you'd expect from someone who wore a full suit even on Saturdays.

Then, in 1923, just as the new Hahnville High School was opening its doors for the first time, the St. Charles Parish School Board came calling. They were building something new—something ambitious—and they wanted Lucien Labry to be a part of it. It was a smart move. He wasn't flashy, but he was the kind of man you could build a school around.

And Hahnville High School—well, it was a sight to behold. The new building was nothing short of magnificent, especially for its time and place. Three full stories, built from a warm yellow-beige brick that stood out against the flat green of the surrounding land. It didn't look like a school so much as a courthouse or a government building. Solid. Permanent. Important.

The entire structure had been raised intentionally, a practical design choice for life along the river. The second level served as the main floor, elevated to avoid the inevitable flooding that came each spring when the Mississippi River, just steps away, began to swell. You couldn't build anything near the river without thinking of high water. The architects had accounted for that. And they did it with style.

The front of the school featured a double circular grand staircase, one that curled gracefully from the ground up to the main entrance on the second floor. It was elegant, almost regal. You could imagine some wealthy plantation owner standing at the top, surveying his land. Only this wasn't a plantation. It was a place of learning.

The two staircases met at a wide landing in the center of the building, where a set of massive wooden doors stood like sentinels. They opened into an equally massive central hallway, cool and dim in the mornings, buzzing with students by midday. From that hall, the building stretched outward—classrooms, offices, interior stairwells that wound their way up to the third floor. Everything about the school felt bigger than life, especially for a boy from Ama who wasn't used to marble steps and brick façades.

For most students, the building itself was impressive. But for me, it also served as a reminder: Mr. Labry ran this place, from the staircases to the athletic fields. And if you found yourself stepping out of line, you didn't just answer to the principal—you answered to family.

All of the windows in the school building were tall and oversized, almost towering, designed with purpose more than style. In those days, before widespread air conditioning, ventilation was everything, especially in the smothering, heavy summers of South Louisiana. The windows stretched high up the walls, inviting every bit of moving air they could catch. When the heat set in—and it always did—they were opened wide to try and pull in even the slightest breeze. It wasn't much, but in that steamy, humid air, any bit of relief mattered.

Walking up to the school each morning, there were two frescoes that you couldn't miss. They were set into the front of the building, positioned with intention, each bearing a quote that was meant to stay with you. And it did. Whether you realized it or not, those words settled into your memory.

One read: "He profits most, who serves best."

The other: "Seek after knowledge and you will be sought."

They weren't just words carved into plaster. Over time, they became a kind of quiet creed for students and teachers alike. You saw them every day—on your way in, on your way out. And somewhere along the way, they started to shape how you thought about the world. Even if you didn't say them out loud, you carried them with you.

The whole building, from its massive staircases to those thoughtful frescoes, stood as a symbol of something larger than itself. It was more than a school. It was a declaration. A brick-and-mortar promise that education mattered in St. Charles Parish. People in the community were proud of it—and they had every right to be. For many families, it was the most impressive building they'd ever stepped foot inside. And standing at the head of it all—stern, pressed, and perfectly poised was Mr. Labry.

You see, in the 1920's and 1930's, high school principals held real authority. They didn't have to run things by a board or hold parent-teacher conferences to justify discipline. When you were on campus, you were under their roof and their rule, and that meant consequences came swiftly—often before you knew what hit you.

Back then, when a student got out of line, the response was direct and unflinching. Corporal punishment was not only allowed—it was expected. And when your principal was also your uncle, you might think that earned you a little grace, a cushion of protection. But you'd be wrong.

Having Mr. Labry as my uncle didn't come with perks. There were no free passes, no winks, no "we'll handle this at home" conversations. If anything, being related to the man made things worse. He held me to a higher standard—his standard—and he didn't hesitate to make an example out of me if I crossed the line. And on the very first day of my freshman year, I did just that.

The fight behind the cafeteria was bad enough. I ended up with a black eye, a bloody lip, a skinned jaw and a few bruised ribs, all thanks to a classmate who had at least three years and a foot on me. But even that wasn't the worst part. The real trouble began when I was summoned to Mr. Labry's office, standing shoulder to shoulder with the very boy who'd just worked me over.

I can still remember that first lunch break, the heat clinging to the school building like a second layer of skin. I'd made a few new friends that morning, boys from a tiny town about nine miles away called Bayou Gauche. They had strong accents, laced with Cajun French, and I could barely keep up with what they were saying. The words rolled out of their mouths like music, smooth and strange, half-English and half-something older.

But I understood enough to know they were good guys. We were laughing, swapping stories, just trying to find a place to sit and eat. We made our way around the east side of the school, hoping to find a sliver of shade. The sun was brutal, high, and hot in the sky, bearing down like it had something to prove. The east wall of the school cast just enough shadow for us to settle in. I was feeling good—hopeful, even. First day of high school. New friends. The air buzzing with possibilities. But that feeling wouldn't last long. Because in just a few short minutes, I'd go from sharing laughs and sandwiches to standing in front of my uncle, bruised, humiliated, and praying that whatever came next didn't involve a call home or worse.

It was at this point—somewhere between the sunshine, the laughter, and the first bite of lunch—that I had my first encounter with Bebe Trosclair. The name sounded harmless, almost friendly, but Bebe was anything but.

He was three years older than me, and already carried the kind of reputation that made other boys step aside without a word. Nobody tangled with him unless they had something to prove—or nothing to lose.

I'd never seen anyone like him. He was the strangest looking human being I'd ever laid eyes on. There was something primitive about him, like nature had rushed the job and left out a few steps in the process. His forehead sloped back so far it looked like his skull had started retreating before his hairline even had a chance. His nose, on the other hand, seemed to have claimed more than its fair share of his face—large, wide, crooked, like it had been broken a few times and never properly reset. But what really caught your eye—was his chin, or lack of it. His lower jaw just stopped short, as if someone forgot to finish carving it.

Some folks, when they were feeling brave, called him Tortue—which I was later told meant turtle in Cajun French. But never to his face. Not unless they had a death wish. I don't think Bebe knew about the nickname, or maybe he did and just pretended not to. Either way, no one dared test him on it.

That day, he was walking by with his girlfriend, who matched him in appearance in the strangest of ways. She had the same hollow eyes, same sharp angles, same off-kilter walk that made you wonder if she, too, had been carved out of rougher clay than the rest of us. They looked like a pair made by fate or by accident, but either way, they fit together.

I wasn't bothering anyone. Just standing with my new friends from Bayou Gauche, still chuckling over something one of them had said, when Bebe veered directly toward me. Without a word, without even looking at me, he slapped the books clean out of my hands. Before I could bend down to pick them up, he kicked them—hard—sending them flying into the gravel of the parking lot. My brand-new schoolbooks, now skidding across oil stains and loose gravel. I just stood there for a second, stunned, trying to figure out if I'd imagined it.

My friends backed away, slowly and silently. They didn't say a word. They'd seen this before. They knew what came next. Most of them expected me to back away, too. After all, Bebe was a monster of a boy, again standing at least a foot taller than me, wide-shouldered with a meanness that didn't need an explanation. He wore it on his face, in the way he walked, in the way he seemed to look at people like they were nothing more than something in his way. Nobody challenged the Turtle. Nobody.

But something inside me snapped. Maybe it was the embarrassment. Maybe it was the heat. Maybe I was just too stubborn for my own good. I didn't think. I didn't weigh the odds. I just reacted, like a spring coming loose. Before I even knew what I was doing, my hand had curled into a fist, and I threw it—hard—right into the middle of his face. It was the kind of punch that should have knocked someone back at least a step or two. Should have surprised him, maybe even hurt a little.

But he didn't move. Not an inch. He just stood there, blinking, like a fly had landed on him. Then he slapped me. Not punched—slapped, like I was a misbehaving child. It landed with enough force to rattle my teeth. My ears rang. My balance went sideways. And before I could recover, he was on me.

What followed wasn't a fight. It was a lesson. A blur of fists and dirt and pain that seemed to last forever but in reality not long at all. I hit the ground more than once. I think I tried to swing back, but if I did, it didn't land. I was outmatched, outclassed, and completely at his mercy.

When it was over, as I've already said, I had a bloody lip, skinned jaw, a busted eye, hurt ribs and my shirt—new that morning—was ripped and stained in blotches of blood so bright it looked like I'd been painted with it. The sun was still high, the school still buzzing, and I was standing there in ruins—defeated, but not ashamed. I may have lost, but I didn't back down.

Fortunately for me, there were teachers nearby who witnessed enough of the beatdown to know it wasn't a fair fight. It took more than one of them—two, maybe three teachers—to pull that Neanderthal of a man-child off of me before he did any permanent damage. Bebe wasn't done, either. You could see it in his face. He wasn't finished fighting; he was just being restrained. His breathing was wild, his eyes blazing with the disbelief that anyone had dared to strike him back. He wasn't used to being challenged, especially not by a scrawny freshman with more nerve than sense.

I didn't catch the teachers' names. It was the first day of the semester, and nothing about them suggested they were in a mood for introductions. They didn't ask for mine either. What they did offer—firmly, and without room for negotiation—was a personal escort straight to the principal's office. It was time for another chat with Mr. Labry, principal extraordinaire of Hahnville High School, disciplinarian of all things disorderly, and, lest I forget, my uncle.

I sat there, bruised and sore, trying to control the pounding in my ears while Mr. Labry listened calmly to the facts from the teacher who had pulled Bebe off me. The teacher told it exactly as it happened—which, thankfully, matched my own version word for word.

Mr. Labry didn't say much. He nodded, eyes behind those wire-framed lenses doing what they always did—measuring, evaluating, judging. His expression didn't change. You never knew what he was thinking until he made his decision, and by then, it was usually too late to negotiate.

After the short debriefing, he reached for his pen and scribbled out a note on school letterhead. He handed it to me with surgical precision.

"Have your father meet with us tomorrow afternoon. Four-thirty."

Us.

That word hit me like a second slap to the head. Us. As in me, him, and my father—the holy trinity of regret. Now, there's only one thing worse than punishment, and that's punishment deferred. It gives your imagination time to wander through every worst-case scenario. And mine did. All the way home.

Dad came home late that evening, like he always did. Dirty, exhausted, and hungry. His shirt was still streaked with grease from whatever machine had demanded his time that day, and his face had that worn, pinched look that said he'd given everything he had out there. Like clockwork, he dropped his toolbox by the porch, came inside, and sat down at the head of our big kitchen table—ready to clean up, eat, and wind down in peace.

That was the routine. That was sacred. But not tonight.

Because waiting for him, folded in half and already on the table, was the letter from Mr. Labry. And foolishly, my mother handed it to him before she handed him his one Falstaff longneck. That one bottle of St. Louis' finest was the buffer between the day's chaos and his evening calm. And tonight, he didn't get that buffer before he got Mr. Labry's note.

Why is it—and this must be universal—that when a father gets a letter from school, his first reaction isn't to read it, but to look straight at his wife with that "What the hell is this?" expression? It's as predictable as rain in the spring. I watched it unfold from my seat at the table, quietly praying that maybe—just maybe—Mom would jump in and explain things before he got too far into the letter. But it was too late. His eyes scanned the page. His jaw tightened. That bottle of Falstaff sat unopened.

Whatever slim chance I had of softening the blow with charm or explanation had evaporated the second he read, "Have your father meet with us tomorrow afternoon. Four-thirty. Lucien Labry"

Dad said nothing. Just exhaled, slow and steady, and stared at the letter a moment longer. He wasn't angry—not yet—but the disappointment was there, sitting right behind his silence. And as I mentioned before, time was the one thing my father had too little of. He worked hard—every single day—keeping machinery running for people who couldn't afford to have it break. Now, instead of a quiet evening with Mom and an early bedtime, he'd be sitting in a stiff wooden chair next to me, across from his brother-in-law, at the principal's desk, discussing why his son had thrown a punch at a boy the size of a sugarcane hauler.

I didn't know how that meeting would go, but I knew this much—It wouldn't be quiet. The next day—my second day of high school—I had exactly one objective: stay away from the Turtle. After the beating I took and the consequences that followed, I had no desire to test fate any further. I figured I'd had my fill of first impressions.

But avoiding Bebe Trosclair was only part of the damage control. Thanks to what Mr. Labry generously labeled my poor judgment, hot temper, and "emotional immaturity," I had now earned myself a spot in his disciplinary routine—a policy he'd developed over years of watching teenagers like me come in with their chests puffed and their priorities misplaced.

So for the rest of that week, every day after the final bell rang, I had to report straight to the principal's office. I had a place assigned in the outer office, that was the waiting area just outside the principal's inner sanctum, where the assistant principal, Mr. Williams, sat alongside the school secretaries, and where all disciplinary roads eventually led. There wasn't much to it. A large desk, several stiff chairs for other felons, and one clear instruction: don't talk, don't move, don't even look like you might do either. Just sit and do homework, for a full hour. Every evening.

That first afternoon, I wasn't alone. Four other inmates shared my sentence; each one spaced out across the outer office like little statues of regret. To my left and right were Robert Zeringue, David Folse, Joseph Landry, and Michael Becnel—fellow freshmen, mischief-makers, and now, fellow detainees. Between the five of us, we probably knew every trick in the book. Unfortunately, we'd just been caught using one too many.

Mr. Labry didn't believe in suspensions. Not unless a student was truly out of control. In his view, giving a teenager three days off from school was less a punishment and more a poorly disguised vacation. And he wasn't in the business of handing out holidays to kids who could barely behave through homeroom. He believed—rightly so, I'd come to understand—that you get the behavior you reward. And nothing encouraged bad behavior like being sent home with nothing to do but celebrate your poor judgment.

So there we sat. A row of boys with red ears and bruised egos, heads bent over our books in silence. It wasn't long into the hour when I heard the door creak open. I turned in my seat and looked up—just in time to lock eyes with my father.

He stood there in the doorway, quiet and unmoving, and for a moment, I thought he might just stare me down and walk away. But he didn't. He held my gaze, his expression flat but not unfriendly, and offered a single word in greeting.

"Matthew............not the usual Mattie..........but the ultra-formal Matthew!

That was all. My father wasn't one for wasting words. I used to think he treated language like a rationed resource—as though God Himself had only given him a set number of sentences, and he wasn't about to run out early. But when he did speak, his words carried weight. One word from him could fill the room more than a dozen from someone else.

He wore his usual uniform—khaki pants and a khaki button-up shirt, sleeves rolled, collar slightly faded, and a pack of Lucky Strikes tucked into the front pocket. Few dressed quite like that, not even the men he worked with. But somehow, it suited him. That was how people knew him—from a distance, from behind the wheel of his truck, from the engine room of a sugar mill. It wasn't long before others started dressing like him, too. It started with one or two men, then more. They respected him—not just for his skill with machines but for the way he carried himself. And if imitation truly is the sincerest form of flattery, then my father was flattered daily.

He nodded once, then walked past me without another word. I straightened up in my seat, hands folded tightly in front of me, trying not to think about what was going to happen in the inner sanctum.....the principal's office. I'd made it through one fight. But this next one, with my dad in a room full of authority figures, would be impossible to win.

Daddy knew everyone in the office. The two secretaries and the assistant principal, they all greeted him like an old friend returning from a long trip rather than the father of a student sitting in detention with a bruised and battered face and disciplinary problems. Their warm welcomes didn't feel warm to me. To me, they felt like someone slowly and deliberately driving a stake deeper into an already wounded heart. They laughed, of course. Not with malice, not really, but at my expense all the same. Nothing cruel, just the easy laughter of people who didn't have to live with the consequences of what came next.

Mr. Williams, the assistant principal, was in a fine mood that afternoon. He didn't bother with formality. No "Mr. Labry" from him. Instead, with a grin, he leaned in and said, "Lucien has been expecting you." Not Principal Labry, not Colonel Labry. Just Lucien. Like this was just a casual get-together, not a meeting about me.

Then, with a simple gesture toward the door, Mr. Williams motioned for my father to go right in. Dad gave a small nod, waited for the last chuckle to fade, and then opened the door to Mr. Labry's office and stepped inside.

Now, my assigned study spot—that tiny square of silent penance, was set directly across from all of this. My back was to the principal's door, so I couldn't see anything. I just sat there, stiff as a board, trying not to move or breathe too loudly. My stomach was a tight knot of anxiety, and my heart pounded in my chest like a hammer on steel. And then—I swear on everything holy—I heard laughter.

Not just a chuckle, either. Not the polite kind of laugh you hear when someone makes a dry comment or tells an office-safe joke. No—this was deep, full-bodied, table-slapping laughter, the kind that came from the gut and shook the walls. It was coming from inside Mr. Labry's office. I froze. My pencil stopped moving, my fingers locked in place. What on earth could possibly be funny in there?

Maybe I imagined it. Fear has a way of distorting things, especially when you're sitting there bracing for a sentence that feels like a lifetime in the making. Maybe the ringing in my ears had fooled me. Maybe the sound had come from somewhere else in the building, and my mind had simply put it behind that door. But I swear—I swear on the biscuits my grandmother made every morning—I heard my uncle and my father, laughing.

It made everything worse.

The door to hallway that lead into the outer office was wide open, which struck me as odd, considering school had officially ended almost an hour ago. Yet students kept wandering in and out, peeking through the door like it was the lobby of a movie theater, and someone had whispered that the feature presentation was happening behind Mr. Labry's office door.

Word had gotten out—as it always does in small-town high schools—that a reckoning was underway. My run-in with Bebe Trosclair had already made the rounds, and now my impending execution—as it was surely being dramatized—was the talk of the hour. A small gathering of football teammates had planted themselves just outside the office, angling for a good view or at least a juicy retelling of what was going on inside. I could hear their low laughter, the scraping of shoes against tile, the shuffling of feet, waiting for something dramatic to unfold.

Then, all too quickly, the principal's door to the outer office swung open, and every sound seemed to drop into a low thud inside my chest. My heart took off again—racing faster than when I'd taken that first swing at Bebe.

I loved my dad. I mean that in the deepest, most bone-deep way a boy can love a father. He worked hard, gave more than he got, and never asked for much in return except that we hold our end of the rope. And now, because of me, he had been dragged into this mess—publicly and unnecessarily.

I wasn't afraid of getting punished at home, not really. Sure, the threat of getting "whacked" was there, but that wasn't what tore at me. What got to me—really got to me—was the fact that I'd embarrassed him. That I'd caused him inconvenience, dragged his name through the school office, and made him sit in a place he didn't belong. He didn't deserve that. He deserved better.

As Mr. Labry stepped into the outer office, true to form, his expression hadn't softened one bit. He didn't do smiles. He didn't do calm reassurance. His face carried a permanent scowl that could make a priest confess things he hadn't done. He was followed closely by my father, who offered me no clue—no wink, no raised brow, not even the comfort of a sigh.

"Mattie," Mr. Labry said, his voice clipped and formal. "Your dad and I have been trying to determine what we need to do to impress upon you that you cannot continue to get into these scrapes."

Before I could even open my mouth, he turned his gaze, not to me, but to my row of fellow inmates.

"Mattie... Mr. Zeringue. Mr. Becnel. Mr. Landry and Mr. Folse," he barked. "Turn your chairs around. Now."

I blinked. What?

Could this possibly get any worse? It was bad enough that my dad had to be pulled from his long day and made to sit through a meeting with his brother-in-law about his delinquent son. But now my friends were being dragged into it, too?

I couldn't believe it. I didn't understand it. I thought maybe I'd misheard him. Or maybe he was calling them out for their own misdeeds, some unrelated nonsense. But the tone of his voice said otherwise. This was connected. Somehow, this had become not just my moment of shame, but ours. And the looks on their faces—Robert, David, Joseph and Michael—mirrored my own. Confused. Apprehensive. Mostly just trying to figure out what in the world was happening.

As their chairs scraped against the wooden floor, the noise rose to a kind of awkward crescendo. The sound of wood on wood, sharp and ungraceful, filled the room like the overture to a tragic play. It wasn't subtle. And it wasn't quiet. My friends turned their chairs, yes, but with the kind of exaggerated slowness that spoke to the collective bewilderment in the room. There were five boys more concerned with moving chairs rapidly, than doing so quietly. No one knew what Mr. Labry was planning, but it had all the markings of something they'd still be talking about by next week. All I could think was, whatever this is... it's not going to be good.

As soon as the tempest of scraping chairs and shifting bodies finally died down, and a hushed kind of stillness settled over the office, Mr. Labry turned his attention to the hallway, specifically to the small crowd of football players still lingering just outside the door, pretending not to know what was going on in the office. They leaned against the wall like they were totally unconcerned about the show they expected, had nowhere to be and nothing better to do, arms folded, shoulders slouched, wearing the practiced look of teenage indifference. But Mr. Labry had seen it all before. Too many years, too many schemes. You didn't become a high school principal in Louisiana without learning to see through an adolescent smokescreen.

"Boys. Boys," he said, his voice rising just enough to snap their attention without sounding angry.

"All of you. There in the hall," he barked, this time with the kind of command that expected no resistance.

"You all seem very interested in what's going on here," he continued. "So come on in. Now."

There was a pause, maybe two seconds of hesitation as if they were weighing their options, but that was all. The tone in Mr. Labry's voice made it clear—this was not a request.

"You'll not miss the transfer," he added flatly. "The bus isn't coming back for a while."

With that, they filed in. Some looked sheepish. Some looked amused. But every single one of them entered the room like it was a courtroom drama, and they didn't want to miss the verdict. And just like that, the outer office was full—an unlikely and mismatched cast. There I sat, along with my four co-conspirators, in after-school purgatory, along with my father, Mr. Williams, the school secretaries and Mr. Labry, of course. And now five more members of the Hahnville High football team.

We all looked around, trying to piece together what exactly was happening here. Was this a group sentencing? A motivational talk? A public humiliation? Or was it all of the above? Mr. Labry turned to the assembled group, now packed shoulder to shoulder in a space designed for maybe half that number.

"Boys, I want you to sit here for a few minutes with me," he said, stepping into the middle of the room, "as Mr. Manz shares a story about something he did when he was about your age."

He paused and let the tension build, thicken.

"It nearly cost him his life."

Every eye in the room widened. Heads turned. Even the jocks stopped fidgeting. I felt the change in the room instantly. What had been a curious crowd of students with a front-row seat to someone else's trouble had suddenly become a captive audience.

I blinked. Wait, what?

I turned my head slowly toward my dad, who hadn't said much since he walked in. I had never heard of this story. Not once. And now, right here, in the principal's office, surrounded by teachers and classmates and my own bruised ego, he was going to tell it?

Fifteen years old, and this was how I was finding out my father had once done something wild enough to nearly get himself killed? I felt... I don't know……confused….slightly betrayed….slightly victimized by my own father. Why now? Why this story in front of everyone? If it was so important, why hadn't he told me before? I looked at him again, my face a mixture of curiosity and quiet disbelief.

Mr. Labry, ever the host of this growing symposium, cleared his throat.

"I think all of you know Mattie's father," he began, gesturing toward my dad like he was introducing a guest lecturer. "We've known each other since we were boys. Grew up together on Providence Plantation in Ama. Went to school and church together." Then he added, with a faint trace of sentiment: "He is a close friend."

Friend? I thought. He's your brother-in-law, for crying out loud. You married his sister, Catherine. But of course, Mr. Labry always spoke with formality, even about family.

He turned to my dad. "Paul, how old were you?"

"Fourteen," my dad replied, his brow rising as if the number still surprised him.

"My goodness," Mr. Labry said, shaking his head. "I cannot believe it has been that long."

There it was again. Not "can't believe"—but "cannot." He wouldn't use a contraction if you paid him. It never failed to amuse me. For all his sternness, it was that one little quirk that always got me. He didn't know how to say you're not. He said, you are not.

Can't became cannot.

Don't became do not.

It wasn't even for emphasis. It was just who he was.

Even as the tension built, I found myself stifling a grin. Mr. Labry, in his three-piece suit, holding court with my dad in khakis and grease-stained boots; they may have grown up together, but they were cut from two very different bolts of cloth.

That smile, though—it didn't last. Because I knew whatever this story was, it wasn't going to be told for entertainment. It was a lesson. And I was the reason it had to be taught. Mr. Labry's tone changed, and so did the room. The decibel level of his voice had lifted just enough to pull everyone's attention inward, like a fisherman reeling in his line.

You could feel it—the grip of anticipation. It was thick in the air, like humidity before a summer storm. I looked around the office and took stock of the scene. Mr. Williams had put down his ink pen, his stack of papers untouched now, forgotten in the shadow of whatever was about to unfold. The two school secretaries had stopped typing; hands still poised above keys like they'd frozen mid-task. One of them even slid her chair back slightly, just enough to get a better view.

The five of us who had earned this after-school punishment had finished the mandatory rearranging of furniture and now sat as still as stone. The smirks and sarcasm had evaporated. This was no longer a joke. My football teammates, those jocks who'd shuffled in out of curiosity, now sat along a long wooden bench beneath the towering window on the front wall of the office.

Something was happening. And in the middle of it all—my dad.

Now, I'd seen my father speak to groups before. Folks from around the parish would gather at Providence Plantation, eager to hear him break down what he'd done with the steam crushers in the mill, how he'd tinkered and twisted them into something faster, something better. He spoke with clarity and confidence, explaining the mechanics of motion like a man born to it.

But this—this was different. I sat there and felt something I hadn't expected. Not fear. Not shame. Awe. He was about to share something big. Something personal. And not just with me, but with all of them. And suddenly, my mind raced in a new direction. What if this didn't land the way Mr. Labry hoped it would? What if it fell flat? What if this deeply personal tale failed to impress my classmates, the boys who'd watched me get roughed up by a guy with no chin and a forehead like a stone slab?

If it didn't have weight, if it didn't carry the punch—I might not recover socially. It wasn't rational, and I knew that. But I was fifteen. That's how we thought.

Dad pulled a chair from the side wall and set it directly in front of us all, his back to Mr. Labry's office door. He didn't say much. He just sat, settled in, and gave a small nod. And then—he began.

What follows is, as best I can recall, in his own words.

Hahnville High School

CHAPTER 5

THE CROSSING, SWIMMING ACROSS THE MISSISSIPPI RIVER

"Boys, as I think you know, I grew up about seven miles from here in Ama," my father began, his voice steady, calm—measured the way it always was when something important was coming.

He didn't look around the room to see if they were listening. He didn't need to. Every set of eyes was already fixed on him.

"I loved growing up here. Loved it," he said again, as if saying it twice made it settle deeper. "My days, when I was your age, weren't all that different from yours, I suppose. I went to school, got home, was forced to study—which I didn't much care for—but I did it anyway."

A few boys chuckled, quietly. My father didn't smile. Not yet.

"And once the schoolwork and chores were done, I'd lace up my old boots and run the mile or so down the road to Providence Plantation, just to catch whatever daylight was left so I could be with my dad."

"My father was a mechanic for Mr. Thomas Sanders. The same Sanders I know you've heard about. Mr. Sanders owns Providence, and just about everything, in Ama including the sugar mill. And it was my father's job to keep that mill running, to keep the tractors rolling, the trucks hauling, the engines turning over when nobody else could get 'em to."

He leaned forward just slightly in his chair placing his khaki covered elbows on his khaki covered knees.

"To me, it was the greatest job in the world. Not because it paid well or because it came with prestige—but because it mattered. Every machine that ran, every barrel of sugar that got produced, every crop hauled to the refinery—my dad had his hands in it. And I got to watch that."

I saw a few of the boys nodding now. Some of them came from families that worked the land, too. They understood.

"I'd be down there every evening, crawling under equipment, handing him tools, watching how he moved. When something didn't sound right, he didn't guess what was wrong. He knew. And by the time summer came around, I was there with him from sunup 'till we couldn't see our own fingers."

The room stayed quiet. Even the clock on the wall seemed to tick more softly.

"By the time I was ready to enter high school, I could tear down a tractor engine, clean it out, and rebuild it clean—end to end. It was second nature by then."

He took a breath, his eyes narrowing slightly—not in anger, but in weight.

"It was a good thing I learned early. Because that summer—the summer I turned fourteen—was when my father was killed at Providence."

He stopped. Just for a second or two. But it was enough.

The air in the room shifted. The silence wasn't awkward—it was heavy. Nobody fidgeted. Nobody made a sound. The words had landed, and we all felt them.

He didn't look up. He didn't have to. Every person in that office—from the principal to the secretaries to the football players lined up along the bench—was with him now. No one moved. No one whispered. I sat still, trying to understand what was coming next and why I was hearing it now.

He looked around the room—not to measure his audience, but to make connect with them.

"Great grandparents. Great parents. Mr. Sanders let me stay on at Providence, doing a lot of the same work my daddy used to do. I can't remember how much he paid me back then, but it must've been enough—'cause I sure don't remember ever goin' without."

A few of the boys nodded. That kind of quiet security—where you don't have much, but you also never feel like you are doing without—that landed with them especially now as times were so tough and so many didn't have jobs to go to.

"Now I ain't gonna lie," he said, voice tapering off just a little, "those first few months without my dad were rough. I mean rough. There was so much I hadn't learned yet, so much I thought I understood but didn't. I wanted to be like him. Wanted to be the kind of mechanic he was. Wanted to make him proud, even after he was gone."

He paused there. Not long. Just enough for the truth to settle.

"But I was lucky. Real lucky. The men who worked beside him—his friends, the ones he taught—they took me in. Helped me. Showed me what he'd taught them. So, I kept learning."

He drew in a breath, like he was resetting.

"I missed my friends. I missed school. But, boys, the truth is—we didn't have many choices. Not me, and not my mom or my sister. When my daddy left us, everything changed. We had to make do. We had to move forward. Simple as that."

He waved his hand, lightly dismissing the heaviness that had crept in.

"But that's not the story Mr. Labry asked me to share with you," he said, shifting in his chair. "What I need to tell you now is... something else."

The room grew still again.

"I cannot explain why I did what I did," my dad said quietly. "I cannot tell you what got into me that day or what part of my brain thought it was a good idea."

His voice had changed. Not softer just more intense—heavier.

"I cannot explain why I'd take a risk like that. Why I'd put my life on the line. Why I'd put my mother through what I did. Why I disappeared—for hours."

The word disappeared hung in the air like a thick fog. And just like that, the atmosphere in the room shifted again.

Even I blinked. Disappearance? What disappearance?

My father had never mentioned anything about that. Not once. And now he was just... dropping it in like it was common knowledge?

I turned my head slowly, saw the others reacting just like me—eyes wide, posture straightening. Something serious was coming, and everyone in the room felt it immediately.

The office went silent. Utterly silent. The sound of typewriters hitting their target had stopped. The quiet hum of conversation in the hallway had hushed. Even the phones, once ringing intermittently, now sat still.

The bench creaked faintly as we stopped shifting. My teammates, just minutes ago too cool to care, were now perched like sparrows on a wire—totally absorbed.

A couple of boys who'd been milling in the hall had slipped closer, peering around the doorframe. One of them mouthed the word "disappearance?" to his buddy, eyebrows raised.

My father looked at us all, not to stir drama, but to hold our attention.

"But the fact is—I did. I made a mistake so foolish, so reckless, that even now, I look back and wonder how I ever made it out of it alive. And that's what I want you to hear. So, I'm asking you—just give me a few minutes. Let me tell it to you straight. And maybe, just maybe, you'll carry it with you. Maybe it'll keep you from doing something just as dumb."

"I was fourteen years old. It was September, 1918. My closest friends were T-, Bob Breaux, E.J. Talbot and Keeter St. Amant. I know y'all know those names—good men, all of them. Men who've done right by this parish. But back then... we were just kids."

There was a glimmer of a smile now.

"Back in those days, we were near 'bout inseparable. All of us from Ama, all around the same age, and our folks all worked for Mr. Sanders at Providence Plantation."

He chuckled once, not loudly—just the kind that sneaks up on you when you remember something fondly.

"We'd grab every minute we could when chores were done and work let up. We'd run straight over the levee in front of the plantation and find ourselves at the river, where we'd strip down and dive in. That was our joy. That was our escape."

He paused and looked around the room again.

"Now, if our parents had found out we were swimming in the Mississippi instead of the bayou..." he whistled and shook his head. "Well, we wouldn't have lived to tell the tale. They would've tanned our hides six ways from Sunday."

Laughter rippled through the room—nervous but genuine.

"But we were young. Dumb. Invincible. That's what we thought. Didn't matter if the river was full of whirlpools, or undertows, or ship traffic, or God-knows-what kind of garbage floating beneath the surface. None of that could touch T-Bob, E.J., Keeter, and Paul."

He leaned back just slightly.

"And yes," he added dryly, "I did use the word dumb. 'Cause that's what it was."

I felt every eye slide my way. I could already hear it. Dumb! That word was going to stick like gum on the bottom of a church pew.

Still, it was worth it.

Because Dad had them all—hook, line, and sinker.

"One evening," my dad began again, his tone shifting toward the inevitable, "we were out at the river like we had been a hundred times before. Diving, swinging from ropes tied to the willow trees, splashing, laughing—acting like a pack of fools, same as always."

The boys in the room leaned forward slightly. Even the secretaries had stopped pretending to type.

"The wind that day was blowing hard from the west—real hard. Strong enough to stir up some whitecaps on the surface of the river, turning it into something that looked more like the Gulf on a bad day than our usual muddy swimming hole. But you know how it is—whitecaps just made it more fun. More of a challenge. More of a thrill. We thought it added to the adventure."

He gave a slow nod, like he could still feel that wind on his face.

"The willow trees lining the riverbank—those spindly limbs were nearly sideways in the gusts, flailing like they were caught in a storm. And us? We didn't pay a lick of attention. We just kept playing, sliding, swimming, shouting to each other across the churning water."

He paused.

"And then, someone yelled."

His voice quieted just a little.

"I don't even remember which one of 'em it was. Might've been T-Bob, or maybe E.J., maybe even Keeter. It doesn't matter. I remember the words. That's what stuck."

He let the sentence hang for a moment.

"I dare you to swim across the river."

That was it.

"I dare you to swim across the river," he repeated, softer.

"I dare you to swim across the river," he said again, eyes lowered.

"You hear something like that when you're fourteen—and I don't care how smart you think you are—something happens. Something inside starts moving around, getting all twisted up. I can't tell you why it mattered so much. I can't tell you why I felt like I had something to prove."

He looked out across the room at all of us.

"These were my closest friends. My brothers, really. I would've taken a bullet for any one of them, and I believe with all my heart they would've done the same for me. But for some reason, in that moment—those eight words felt like a commandment. Like God Himself had parted the clouds and handed me a challenge. Like the river was a stage, and I'd just been called up to show what I was made of."

He leaned back in his chair.

"I DARE YOU TO SWIM ACROSS THE RIVER."

He said it louder this time, slow and heavy.

"I DARE YOU TO SWIM ACROSS THE RIVER."

A nervous laugh fluttered through the room, and a few of the younger boys looked around, unsure if it was okay to laugh in Mr. Labry's outer office.

Dad smiled.

"Now boys," he said, eyes twinkling just a bit, "you have to remember something. We were skinny-dipping. I was wearing exactly what I came into this world with."

That brought laughter—real, belly-deep laughter. Even Mr. Labry cracked a smile, which by itself was worth the price of admission.

One of the secretaries—bless her—turned a shade of red not found in nature and buried her face in a page she had no intention of typing. The boys howled. I heard one whisper, "He said it. He actually said it."

Dad shook his head.

"But a dare is a dare. And almost before the words finished echoing off the riverbank, I was off—headed straight for the middle of the Mississippi River, no clothes, no plan, and no sense. Just hootin' and hollerin' from the shore behind me."

He mimicked their voices:

"YOU'LL NEVER MAKE IT ACROSS!"

"TELL THE GIRLS HELLO WHEN YOU GET TO NEW ORLEANS!"

"YOU SURE GOT A WHITE BUTT!"

The office erupted again. The secretaries doubled down in their typewriters, practically hugging them like shields. I could barely keep from laughing myself, even though I was sure this story was going to haunt me later in the locker room.

Dad waited for the noise to die down.

"And I swam. I was moving hard, my arms cutting through the muddy water, head down, focused. But pretty quickly, I realized something. I wasn't just swimming away from shore—I was drifting fast. The current had me, and I was getting pulled downstream before I'd even made it thirty yards."

He paused again. The room stilled.

"I turned my head, looked back—and I couldn't see my friends anymore. Just the gray-brown swells of the river and the willows blowing in the wind. The bank was gone. I wasn't where I thought I was, and I sure wasn't in control."

"I treaded water, trying to spot anything familiar, trying to judge how far I'd come—and it hit me."

He spoke slower now.

"There was no one around. Not a soul. Just wind, and water, and the whispering of the trees. I was out there all alone, and it dawned on me like a freight train—I'd messed up."

His voice lowered even further, his eyes not focused on anyone anymore.

"There was no one to see me make it across. No one to cheer. No one to hand me a medal. No one to hoist me on their shoulders. No one even knew where I was anymore."

He held up a hand as if ticking off thoughts one by one.

"There was no one to help me if I got in trouble.

There was no one to see me fail.

There was no one who could find my body if I didn't come back."

And then the line that sat with all of us:

"There it was. Fail. That word. That truth. That terrifying realization that maybe—just maybe—I wouldn't make it back."

He looked down at the floor.

"That was when it hit me, deep in my chest. Not fear exactly—humility. I realized that what I was doing wasn't brave. It wasn't bold. It was stupid. It was dangerous. And it could kill me."

"Boys, I want you to understand something," my dad said, and his voice had changed again—lower now, not with drama, but with something heavier. "I've never felt my pulse like that before. Never. Not before, not since."

He didn't fidget. He didn't blink. He just told it, clean and straight.

"I was fourteen years old. I could run the mile from our house to Providence Plantation in minutes. Did it often enough that I didn't think twice about it. But right then—in the middle of that river—my heart felt like it was trying to climb out of my chest."

He pressed a hand to his temple.

"I could feel the veins in my head throbbing. In my forehead, right here along the side of my face—pounding. Not beating. Pounding. Like I was trapped on train tracks and a freight engine was bearing down and I couldn't even lift a finger to move."

He looked at each of us in turn.

"I was scared," he said quietly. "Really scared. And I finally knew—too late almost—that I had to turn around and get back to that west bank, back to where I'd started."

The room was still. Even the air felt still.

"I hadn't thought about the current. I hadn't thought about the undertows or the river trash or the whirlpools. But when I put my head down and started swimming back to the west bank where this misadventure had begun. I swam with everything I had, I realized something awful."

His voice faltered slightly.

"I wasn't in control anymore. Not of where I was going. Not of how fast. The current had me. It had me good. And no matter how hard I tried—how deep I dug—I couldn't fight it. I couldn't get back. I was being pulled farther and farther from where I'd started and dragged right into the belly of that river."

He shook his head slowly.

"Looking around, I couldn't tell where I was, not that it mattered. The only things I could see were two levees, a mess of wind-whipped willow trees, and the occasional sandbar. I was lost out there in a world I'd known my whole life—but now it was different. Now it was hostile."

"I guessed I was about two hundred yards from the bank. Not that far if you're running it. But in that water, with that current, it might as well have been a thousand miles. And I was still being pulled deeper, faster, farther into the middle of the river."

He blinked, then added, almost as if to himself:

"I started to panic. Not just worry—panic. I couldn't tell if those were tears rolling down my face or just more of that dirty river water. I didn't know if I was crying or drowning."

No one moved. No one breathed.

"And then," he said, his voice tightening, "I heard it. Two short blasts of a tugboat horn. Loud. Close. Closer than I ever wanted to hear something like that."

He stopped. The pause was deafening.

"I turned, tried to wipe the muck from my eyes. And when I looked up, I saw it. I saw an enormous wall of rusted steel, black with river grime and oil, barreling toward me. A series of barges, lashed together like a floating city block, being shoved downriver by a tug. And the current wasn't slowing it down—it was speeding it up."

He let the image sit in our minds.

"I'd seen those barges my whole life, standing on the banks with my dad. I'd watched them push through the turns, pass in front of the levee. I knew—knew—that the pilot up there couldn't see a kid in the water. Not from that high up. Not with all that cargo in the way."

He stared at the wall for a second, and then back to us.

"He wasn't looking for me. He didn't know I was there. He was watching for channel markers, for other ships. He wasn't watching for some dumb fourteen-year-old boy bobbing naked in the river."

"I knew what was coming," he said. "And worse than that, I knew I couldn't stop it. The current had me locked in and the strong winds from the west didn't help as they continued to push me farther and farther into the main channel of the river. The water wasn't listening. My arms were moving, kicking, flailing—but I may as well have been swimming in quicksand. Nothing I did made a difference. Nothing. The river was making the decisions now. I swam toward the west bank of the river where this journey had begun and got nowhere. I swam towards the east bank and got nowhere."

His eyes looked out past us like he could still see it coming.

"The wind had picked up even more, throwing waves over my head, slapping me in the face. I couldn't see. Couldn't breathe without sucking in mouthfuls of river water. I couldn't tell which way was out. And for the first time in my life—really the first time—I thought I might not make it. I really thought that might be the end."

Then, softer:

"And in the middle of all of that, with this massive wall of steel headed right toward me, I thought about my mom. Not because I could hear her voice. Not because I thought she'd come rescue me. But because I realized—if something happened to me out there, if I didn't come back—she'd never know what happened. She'd just wait. And wait. And hurt."

He looked down at his hands.

"I'd never felt shame like that. Not fear—shame. Because I was the one who did this. To her. To me. To everyone."

"Booonnncckkkk, Booonnncccckkkk!!!"

The sound blasted through the room like a thunderclap, and for a half-second, I thought someone had dropped a stack of textbooks or maybe set off a firecracker. But no—it was my dad. His voice, sudden and booming, had startled every single person in that packed outer office. The secretaries jumped. The boys flinched. Mr.

Williams even dropped the pen he was holding. For a moment, it felt like the whole room had been struck by lightning.

Then came the laughter. Nervous, awkward, startled laughter. The kind that bursts out when you don't know what else to do. The boys broke into chatter, some still wide-eyed, others chuckling under their breath, all momentarily shaken by my father's spontaneous cannon blast.

"The southbound barge sounded its horn," Dad said, nodding slowly, "and it was right on top of me."

His voice was quieter again, but every ear in the room was locked in.

"I was dead center in front of the barge when it started drifting, slowly, toward the east bank—its port side."

He turned to me.

"Mattie, son, I've never—never—been so scared in my life."

"Thank the Lord, that tug was shifting course, turning away from me. But even as it turned, I knew why."

He leaned forward slightly in his chair.

"When a ship gives two short horn blasts, it's signaling that it's turning left, to it's port side. That's standard on the river. But more importantly—that signal only happens when there's something in the way. Usually, it's another ship, another barge, coming in the opposite direction. And boys, let me tell you—when one mountain of steel is headed toward you, the last thing you want is another one coming up behind you."

You could hear a pin drop in the room.

"I tried to turn around, just to look, to confirm what I already knew deep in my gut. But I couldn't. I physically couldn't make myself look. It's like my neck locked up. My body wouldn't let me turn, wouldn't let me see it. I guess... I thought if I didn't look, it wouldn't be real. Like maybe if I ignored it, those barges would just vanish."

His voice dipped low.

"But they didn't vanish."

He let the silence hang.

"Booonnncccckkkk, Booonnnccccckkkk!!!" he mimicked again—softer this time, like an echo.

"And sure enough, from behind me, I heard it—another set of horn blasts. Muffled by the river, by the wind, but there all the same. Another set of barges was headed upriver. I knew it. I knew it before I heard it, and now I couldn't un-hear it."

His breathing slowed, but his eyes didn't move.

"Boys, I can't explain to you what I felt in that moment. Panic wasn't even the word. I was shaking, inside and out. I couldn't catch my breath. The water was battering me from every direction, and I was hyperventilating on top of it. My chest hurt from fear."

He paused.

"And then the worst thought hit me again. What if they didn't turn fast enough or what if I was smack in the middle of that invisible space between their paths, and the river decided to throw me right under one of them?"

His voice dropped to a whisper.

"I thought about my mom again."

That was all he said. And that was all he had to say.

"I wanted to scream. I think I might have. I don't remember if I said it in my head or out loud but—'Momma!' That's what came out."

He let out a deep breath.

"And the noise. Lord, the noise. The horns. The pounding of the tug engines. The roar of the water as the bows of those barges cut through the river like knives. The whole river shook. You could hear it, but more than that, you could feel it—through your chest, through your ribs, like the water itself had come alive."

"The barges heading south were now fully headed to their port side. The ones heading north? Same thing. And me? Right in the middle. Caught between two convoys of steel, in a mess of brown water, boiling water around me."

He shook his head, still amazed.

"I don't know how it happened, boys. Maybe it was luck. Maybe it was the river being merciful. But those barges, those mountains of steel—they parted. Just enough. Like something pushed them to either side. And there I was, alone in the middle, maybe twenty yards between them in either direction, with waves crashing over me, engines thundering, horns still crying out in the air."

He looked down, suddenly quiet.

"It wasn't the parting of the Red Sea. But it was close enough for me."

He leaned back in his chair.

"I tried to count how many barges were lashed together. Tried to figure out how long this ordeal might last. But I couldn't see. The river kept tossing me. I heard more than I saw. And even then—what difference did it make? One barge or twenty, there was nothing I could do. Nothing except stay afloat and pray."

He glanced around the room again.

"I started to think about the propellers. You know what I mean? If I drifted too close, they'd suck me in like a rag doll. I thought about the one in front of me. The one behind me. I thought about whether I'd feel it when it happened, or if it'd be really fast."

His voice dropped to almost a whisper.

"Would I make it as they passed me?

Would they pull me under?

Would they let me go?

Would they hold me down until..."

He didn't finish the sentence. He didn't have to.

"I was tossed around like a rag doll," my dad continued, his voice heavy with the memory. "The wakes from both ships slammed into each other right where I was, turning the river into a boiling mess. The whitecaps were taller now, whipped up by the strong west wind and churned by the passing barges. I tried to get a breath—just a single, clean breath of air—but every time I surfaced, another wave crashed into my face."

"I was coughing, sputtering, struggling not to inhale the filth around me. And make no mistake, boys, the Mississippi River ain't no swimming hole. That water was brown, thick, full of debris and God-knows-what. It tasted like diesel and rot. My eyes burned. My lungs felt like they were on fire. Each time I got a gulp of air, it was mixed with river. I was panicked, flailing, unable to catch my rhythm, unable to find the surface for more than a moment before the next wave smacked me down."

His eyes moved across the room slowly, pausing on each boy as he spoke.

"I could hear those engines still pounding, louder than thunder, echoing through the water like beating drums. And under the surface? Even worse. The sound didn't go away under there—it got trapped. The thud of the pistons was muffled but still deafening, like the river itself was shaking with every cycle."

He took a deep breath.

"Thing was, the two barges weren't moving at the same speed. The one heading to Baton Rouge—northbound—was slower, fighting the river's current. It crawled past me, dragging out the nightmare. The southbound tug had already passed, but its wake was still slapping me from behind. I was caught in the middle, getting battered from both ends. My arms were noodles. My legs were rubber. There was nothing left. I was trying to keep my head above water, but the fight was draining out of me fast."

He paused again, eyes distant.

"I remember praying, hoping that someone on one of the tugs would see me. Just spot me for a second, throw a line, something. But I was invisible. Just a speck in a river full of motion. No one saw me."

"I kept swallowing water. I couldn't stop coughing. I couldn't breathe right. My belly started to bloat from all the river water I'd swallowed. My limbs ached. And for the first time in my life, I felt helpless. Completely helpless. That river was going to decide what happened to me. It was totally in charge now."

He leaned forward again, quieter now.

"I called for her again. 'Momma!' I screamed it out, not even thinking about who could hear me. It just came out—like a reflex. My voice was hoarse from coughing, but I yelled anyway."

"And then, as if the devil himself had planned the moment, the wakes from both barges met exactly where I was. They didn't blend. They collided. The brown water foamed and bucked like a wild animal. I was caught in it—pounded from both sides, flipped upside down more times than I could count. I couldn't even tell what was up anymore. I was coughing, choking, spinning. Every time I surfaced, the river smacked me back down like it wasn't done with me yet."

"I couldn't breathe. I couldn't scream. I couldn't even pray anymore—not out loud, at least. All I could do was think. Think about Mom. About home and Mom's warm kitchen. About the little round rug by the radio where I used to sit and listen to the radio. I just wanted to be there again. I didn't want to die in this cold, brown hell."

He swallowed, and for a moment, his voice wavered.

"I remember how cold I was. So cold. Not just from the water, but from fear, exhaustion, everything. It had gotten darker too. I hadn't noticed how quickly evening was coming until I looked up, hoping to see something—anything—that would give me hope. Instead, the sky gave me nothing. Just gray, heavy clouds and the creeping chill of night. The realization hit me like a punch—I might not make it out of this. And if I didn't, no one would even know where to look."

Silence swept across the room like a tide.

"My journey downriver continued, slower now that the barges had passed, but no less frightening. The water was still churning, the wind still howling. Then, out of the corner of my eye, I saw something—a blur of structure on the west bank."

He straightened up slightly.

"It was the ferry landing in Luling."

For the first time in a while, there was a collective breath in the room.

"I couldn't tell how far I was from it at first, but as I turned my head, I could see the Destrehan side too, and I realized I was closer to the east bank. My heart jumped. Maybe this was it—my way out."

"I put my head down and swam as hard as I could. Every stroke was agony. My muscles were jelly, my lungs raw, but I swam. I didn't look up until I had to, until I thought my lungs would explode. I was afraid that I was making little or no progress. And when I did finally look up, the ferry landing was behind me. I'd missed it."

A wave of disappointment passed over his face.

"I kept swimming, thinking maybe I could fight the current and those strong west winds that seemed to be getting stronger. But there was no fighting it. The river had other plans. I had no choice but to stop. I just treaded water, letting it carry me wherever it wanted. The Gulf of Mexico? Maybe. I didn't know. I didn't care. I was too tired to fight. Too tired to cry."

He looked down at his hands.

"That's when I prayed again. Not the kind of prayers you say in church. Not the ones you mumble because it's Sunday. This was different. This was a plea. A cry. A bargain. 'God, if I don't make it, just… let them find my body.'"

His voice caught. He didn't say anything else for several seconds and that pause had impact.

"Boys, about four miles below Ama," my dad said slowly, as if tracing the route in his mind, "the river takes a hard bend to the southwest. Now if you're headed downstream like I was, that would mean the river bends to the right and the current begins to move to the left side or east bank of the river. And after years of replaying every second of that night in my mind, I've come to believe that bend is what saved me.

He glanced around the room, his voice steady but still heavy from the weight of memory.

"That bend in the river, along with the wakes from those barges and the strong westerly winds, pushed me farther and farther toward the east bank. I didn't know it at the time, but all of it—the current, the bend, the wind, the chaos—was nudging me in the only direction that might offer a way out."

He paused, let that hang a moment, then went on.

"By then, the shoreline had disappeared from view completely, except for those ferry landings that I passed...... what felt like hours ago. The water was all I could see. Just water and the sky and, now and then, the willows—those long, narrow branches dancing in the wind, dipping toward the river like they were trying to touch it. I watched them. I prayed for them. I begged the river to carry me to one of those branches."

He was speaking faster now, not in a rush, but with urgency—like someone running out of breath and time at once.

"If the current could just carry me a little closer...

If the willow branches kept dipping down to the surface...

If I could just grab one—just one—that didn't whip out of reach...

If I could find the strength to hold on long enough to stop...

If the bank wasn't so high above the water line...

If the current didn't pull me so fast...

If I had just a second more."

"The muddy river kept dragging me closer to the east bank. I didn't know it, but I was getting near the cut bank down below Destrehan. The river narrows slightly there, and the current speeds up. It was moving fast now—faster than ever—and I was still trying to kick, trying to stay afloat. My arms were numb. My legs—like deadweight. Cold, useless, like they weren't even mine. I couldn't feel my toes anymore. I tried to swim, but all I could do was drift and kick weakly now and then just to keep my head above water."

"I was barely living. I wasn't really alive—I was just surviving. I had no idea how long I'd been out there, but I knew I couldn't last much longer. It had been hours. It felt like days. The river wasn't letting go, and I had nothing left to give."

He looked around again. No one spoke. Not a breath stirred the room.

"And then," he whispered, "after what felt like an eternity, I felt something soft brush against my cheek."

"It was a willow branch."

"The current and the wind had finally brought me into a mess of them—a whole curtain of willow limbs, thin and swaying, reaching down from the trees like they were searching for me too. They swept across my face, my shoulders, my arms, like a thousand fingers reaching out."

"I tried to grab one. Just one. But my hands… my fingers were stiff and lifeless. Like frozen wood. They wouldn't close. They wouldn't hold."

"I couldn't even feel them."

His voice dipped lower. "And then, out of nowhere, the current slammed me sideways into a thick limb—jagged and gnarled, like it had broken off in a storm. It hit me hard, stabbing me in the ribs on my right side. It felt like an axe had chopped through me. I couldn't breathe. The pain shot through my whole body. I curled up instinctively—just folded into myself because the pain was too much. I wasn't thinking about the river anymore. I wasn't thinking about the current or the barge or even home. I was just thinking about how much it hurt."

Dad's hand went to his side.

My chest felt like it was collapsing in on itself. Breathing was no longer just painful—it was impossible. My face slipped under the water again and I barely managed to lift one arm. Just one arm as I tried in desperation to grab one willow limb……..just one."

He paused again. The room was silent.

"I lifted my left arm out of the water using it like a line…… like a fisherman casting out one last time before the storm. I had nothing left. No pride. No bravado. Just desperation. Just hope."

His voice broke slightly.

"I whispered, 'Please, God. Just let me catch something.'"

"I didn't shout. I didn't scream. I couldn't scream. But inside, I was yelling. Begging. Crying out like I never had before. 'Help me grab something, Lord. Help me find a way out of this.'"

He looked down now, quieter still.

"Momma," he whispered.

Dad paused for a moment and slowly uncrossed his legs. Again, Dad anchored his greasy khaki covered elbows on this khakis coved knees as he leaned forward. He wasn't just talking now—he was reaching for us, drawing the circle tighter.

"Boys…" he started, then glanced around at the swelling crowd gathered in the outer office. "Now boys and girls…"

The office was full—my classmates, the football players, the transfer driver, the secretaries, even Mr. Williams were waiting impatiently for my dad to continue. All eyes were on my father. He scanned the room deliberately, trying to meet every gaze, holding it for just a second longer than expected, like he wanted to be sure that each person knew this wasn't a story anymore. This was testimony.

"Most of you know me," he said evenly. "You all know I'm a God-fearing man. You see me every Sunday at Holy Rosary. You know I work hard, and I do my best to live an honest life. My name, my word—they matter to me. I wouldn't lie—not now, not ever."

He straightened a little but didn't break his posture. "What I'm about to tell you is the truth. It's the same thing I told Sheriff Vicknair when they found me and brought me to the hospital. Word for word. I'm going to tell you exactly what happened, as best as I can remember it, and I need you to listen with open minds and open hearts. This ain't made up. It's not exaggerated. It's what happened."

The room shifted with a ripple of quiet murmurs and exchanged glances, but no one spoke. Heads nodded. Eyes stayed locked. The sense of reverence was unmistakable. Even the transfer driver stepped in fully now, hat in hand, standing among the crowd, sensing what we all did—that something sacred was about to be said.

My dad glanced at Mr. Labry. And in return, the principal gave a small, solemn nod. His brow arched in quiet approval, as though giving an official blessing for Dad to continue.

My dad took a breath and began again.

"Boys, as the current dragged me along the east bank of the river, I was finished. Cold to the bone. My muscles no longer obeyed me. My ribs—busted up from hitting that log—felt like they'd been cracked with a baseball bat. Breathing wasn't just painful, it was almost impossible. My chest ached with every shallow gasp."

He clenched his side as he spoke, the pain, indelibly etched in his memory.

"I was completely spent. I wasn't thinking straight anymore. Everything looked hazy—the sun had set behind the levee on the west bank, and it was getting darker. My vision was blurring. Something in that dirty water must've gotten in my eyes, burning like the devil. I couldn't see. I couldn't breathe. I was just a body moving where the current took me."

He closed his eyes for a second, not in drama, but as if remembering it clearly, too clearly.

"And that riverbank on the east side—it might as well have been a cliff. The river was running low from the long dry summer, and that bank stood three, maybe four feet above the waterline. Sheer and slick with sand and mud. No foothold. No roots. No handholds. Just wet, loose dirt and hopelessness."

"I tried—Lord knows I tried. I kept reaching for those willow branches, thinking maybe, just maybe, one of them might hold. But they snapped like twigs in my hands. My palms were shredded from the struggle, scraped raw. All I had to show for it were fingers full of green, useless willow leaves."

His voice dropped, and he stared at the floor.

"I couldn't pull myself up. I couldn't hold on. I had no breath left. My legs were dead weight. My arms, noodles. My ribs stabbed at me with every twitch. The mud was too slick, the bank too high, and I had nothing left to give. I continued to lift one arm out of the muddy water in search of a limb to grasp"

"I had taken what I knew were my last breaths."

He paused, not dramatically, but because it was hard to say.

"I stopped fighting," he said quietly. "Right there in the river, I let go. I wasn't afraid anymore. I wasn't angry. I wasn't sad. I just… gave in. And as I drifted, the cold seeping into my bones, the stars starting to show up overhead, I remember thinking, 'It's over.'"

Silence.

The outer office was still. Not even a shuffle of feet or a creak of wood. The students, the teachers, the secretaries, the transfer driver, Mr. Williams—every one of them frozen in place. Not a sound came from the hallway. There was total silence as everyone listening was totally focused on my dad.

And then my father said, again—so soft we barely heard it.

"It was over."

CHAPTER 6

MR. ROBOTTOM

"My lungs were about to explode … my whole body was numb from exhaustion and from the frigid waters of the river, when something grabbed my left wrist. My arm that was still extended out of the water, and still searching for a miracle, was grabbed by some force stronger than any man's grip that I have ever felt. Something grabbed my left wrist and at the same time pulled me out of the river in one powerful motion. My left shoulder felt like it was being torn from its socket as unimaginable pain shot through crushed ribs and now my left shoulder. My rib cage on my right side that had been sandwiched by the end of that large tree trunk along the shore a few moments before, now hurt beyond description. Breathing now was doubly difficult because of fatigue and my busted ribs and a dislocated shoulder.

"Before I realized what had happened, I hit the sandy loam of the riverbank and cried out in horrific pain as I landed on my bruised, busted ribs and dislocated shoulder. I literally cried when I hit the sand. I hurt everywhere and the fact that I was safe and out of that damned… sorry, Lucien, Mr. Labry, sorry, ladies, boys… that sorry river was no consolation… The pain was so sharp, so deep, it knocked whatever air I had left straight out of me. I was safe—technically—but at that moment, it didn't feel like a rescue. I curled up like a baby, partly because I was cold, some because I was in such pain, and mostly because I was still scared to death."

"It took a moment before I realized that I was out of the river.

"I heard a loud scream...... an almost panicked voice, "Boy, what da hell ya doing in dat river?" "Is you crazy?

"The room exploded in laughter....... nervous laughter to be sure, but the way my dad mimicked the voice of the man who had saved his life was comical. The secretaries and Mr. Williams were now totally captivated by Dad's story and no longer reacted timidly to the occasional colorful language. They seemed to realize that, though unusual for the setting, it was also harmless. There had been such tension in the room and though we all knew that my dad's presence alone meant that he did not die in the river, we still had followed the tale so closely that we still weren't certain how it might end.

"'Aww, my shoulder, my chest...' Dad said, coughing between words. 'I think you broke my shoulder!' I cried.'

" Ya shoulda, ya chest? Boy what 'about ya butt? Damn, boy? What ya do? You dun fall oft of one of those big ships, the man screamed"? "They workin' on dem ships nekkit, na? "That just did it. Laughter erupted again, this time louder. Even the secretaries, who had earlier tried their best to keep a straight face, were chuckling now. Dad had pulled us all back from the edge of that river with his humor, the same way this stranger had pulled him from the water.

"Hell, I was just sittin' by the river minning my own bizness and fishin' for some river catfish fo' my dinna and you come floating bye and I gotta fish you outta dat river instead. He screamed in an almost panicked voice.

"I didn't fall off no boat," I cried.

"Who, who are you," I asked.

"Who am I? Who am I? I'm the dummy that just pulled your sorry nekkit butt outta the river, how do you do," he roared in response to my question."

'Folks call me Robottom. Don't need no other name. Just Robottom,' he said, as if that settled everything. 'Well, I know ya ain't fell outta the sky! Boy, ya almost scare me white!' he howled, shaking his head.

"The room burst into another round of laughter as my dad mimicked the booming voice and wide-eyed disbelief of the man who'd saved him. Even the secretaries were now completely drawn into the story, smiling freely.

"Dad kept going. 'Robottom picked me up like I weighed nothing. I cried out in pain—it felt like every nerve in my ribs and shoulder caught fire when he hoisted me off the ground. He was careful, sure, but even careful hurt like hell. He carried me maybe twenty yards or so, his arms strong and steady, and gently set me down beside the warmest, most beautiful fire I had ever seen in my life. Before I could say a word, he tossed a few more pieces of driftwood onto the blaze, like he'd been waiting for company to visit all along. I laid down next to that warm fire trying desperately to get warm.

"Then Robottom knelt beside me and wiped my face with something—maybe an old rag, I don't know—but whatever it was, it came away black with river oil and muck. I must've looked like I'd been dragged behind a coal cart. After that, he handed me something in an old, dented tin cup. I took a sip and almost instinctively nearly spit it halfway across the batture. Wine? It tasted like it had been brewed in an old boot. "My friends in the room couldn't help themselves and burst out laughing. None of us drank, not really, but we'd all snuck a taste of wine before and remembered exactly how awful that first sip was. They were just glad my dad didn't stop the story to ask how they knew we didn't like wine.

"Now guys, I was laying there in such pain looking at the face of a colored man I had never seen before. His face was somewhat blurred by the smoke, and fire that, now separated the two of us. In fact, other than the deep almost guttural voice of this stranger, the only other sound that I was aware of, was the sound of something being fried in a tiny skillet over that open fire, the cracking and popping sounds offered by the little fire itself as well as the wind racing through the leaves of the nearby willow trees. The wind that had generated whitecaps on the river was blowing stronger and aided in keeping the blaze of firewood burning brightly. Even as I lay there dazed and totally confused, I was alert enough to realize that whatever he was preparing in the tiny, soot-covered pan, smelled wonderful and, I guess, all the excitement, the exertion and time in that cold, dank water had affected my appetite. I was hungry.

"He had introduced himself as Robottom and he had to ask me for my name. I wasn't being rude, I was still trying to deal with my ribs, the bloodied palm of my hand that I had shredded when I attempted to grab the willow branches, the throbbing pain of my busted left shoulder, and the indignity of laying in front of a total stranger wearing only a frown. Even though I was lying next to a warm fire, I was still freezing, exhausted and still scared about what I had just put myself through......and I was totally confused as to how I had ended up laying down next to a fire with this old colored man.

"I could not help but laugh at the way my dad had described the scene. I found it amusing, but I also thought that I had the greatest dad in the world. Thank goodness the guys liked my dad's story.

"Dad continued, "I had no idea how old Robottom was, but he was advanced in age and what hair was left on his half-bald and massive, round head and his full, beard was almost white. He had a very wide nose, and his nostrils were flared making his nose the most dominant feature of his face. His lips were very large, proportioned to his nose... wide, thick and dark, really dark, but partially covered by his unkept beard. His skin was as black as the iron skillet he was cooking with, and he had no teeth that I could see...

"I don't have any recollection of the clothes he was wearing, except that I know he had a coat because he placed it around me shortly after he carried me from the riverbank to the place where I was lying beside the fire. In fact, the only features I remember seeing in the darkness that had surrounded us were his massive, calloused hands and his face. I wasn't at all afraid of him. He had a kind demeanor about him, and I guess, it would be difficult to be afraid of a man who had just fished me out of a river, carried me, clothed me, cleaned my face and given me something to drink. Robottom cleaned my face as he said it was covered in oil, mud and sand. I began to relax a bit about Robottom, but not about my condition.

"Acchh…I hate wine…if that can be called wine," I cried.

Robottom laughed at me and said," It can be called wine, it is wine. Ya sho is choosey considerin' ya aint got much to choose from out here."

"And I might be crazy, but I ain't the one laying nekkit on the side of the river freezing his pink litta ass oft," he preached, again laughing at my expense and predicament.

"The secretaries now looked on with smiles of approval as the shock of this continued "vulgarity" (especially in mixed company and in the principal's office, no less), had diminished with its frequency of use.

"I'm okay just leave me alone, okay?" I said and regretted it immediately.

"Leave ya alone," Robottom yelled.

"Boy juss two seconds ago ya was screamin' fa me to pull your pink butt outta that water. I pull ya out, and I can kick ya butt back in," he said. He thought this was funny and his laughter was like thunderclap rolling through the batture.

"Please…," I whined.

Robottom stood and walked around the fire towards me and said, " Look at ya' han' boy. What did ya do? Ya bleeding like a stuck pig." I looked at the palm of my hand and even through blurred vision could easily see that it was shredded and bloody.

"I guess that's from the willow branches," I said, "I was tryin' to grab them..."

"Still crouched beside me, he took the same grimy cloth he'd used on my face and dipped it into a nearby bucket of muddy river water. "Here. Let me wrap this 'round ya hand to stop it bleedin.'" The cloth was rough, but his touch was gentle. He folded the fabric around my hand with surprising precision, his calloused fingers working with the skill of a man who had treated plenty of wounds before—probably his own. He wasn't in a rush. He was careful. He was kind. And when he stood up, he tugged his coat tighter around my shoulders like a mother would a child.

"Robottom walked back around to the other side of the fire and continued cooking his meal as he deftly wielded a willow branch to carefully maneuver whatever he was cooking in his black charred pan. The meal had been frying, unattended now, for several minutes and Robottom was more than aware of that. The flames from the fire indiscriminately illuminated different parts of his face as he focused on his meal he was frying over the intense, glowing fire. The night now perfectly framed his face.

"Dis is good river catfish, caught this evening just befo' I caught your silly, pink butt," he said. Somehow, he managed to get a small piece of fish between two willow twigs and was bringing it up to his mouth to taste when he stopped and asked, "How old ya, boy?"

"I'm 20," I lied.

"He froze before he could take a bite and looked at me with disbelief. Then he howled, a full-throated cackle that echoed off the massive levee and because he was paying more attention to my lie than he was to his "eating," he burned his mouth on the piping hot fish he was trying to eat and that he had just taken out of the hot, greasy frying pan. He let the hot fish fall from his mouth into his massive hands which he shook violently, bouncing the fish in his palm as if that was going to cool it off, but as it continued to burn his fingers and lips, he finally, let the fish fall from fingertips back into the frying pan."

"Twenty years old, huh," he questioned. "And tell me, ya is married with tree chillren," he added mockingly.

"It was obvious that Robottom did not believe my lie and I could see him smiling and shaking his head through the smoke and flames from the banquet he was preparing. I thought of my mom and how she would not be very proud of me for lying. She taught me better.

"Woohoo," Robottom yelled as he handed me a piece of fish wrapped in a piece of thin corn bread. As I reached for the fish, my shoulder reminded me of how much it hurt.

"Dis ain't da best food I eva taste but dis fish look and smell a lot betta den what you AIN'T eatin.' It ain't non of dat fancy Na Awlin cazeen, but we ain't in Na Awlins............and there ain't no way they'd serve your nekkit little butt, no how, he added as his eyes squinted while a broad smile spread across his toothless, coal-black, gray whiskered face as his focus returned to his river cuisine. "

"My friends sat mesmerized and hanging on every word. I had never heard my dad tell a story like this, but I was so proud of the story and my dad's effort at telling it to us. I had no idea if this was all true or exaggerated, but I loved every second. My dad was a celebrity, and I was, of course, famous by association. Mr. Labry continued standing very formally, erect, almost nobly by Dad's side, while Mr. Williams and the school secretaries continued to listen intently…taking full advantage of this time away from filing, typing and other office chores.

"As offered earlier, I had never eaten fish before and Mr. Robottom's kindness had placed me in a difficult position. There was no way I wanted to eat that fish, but there was no way that I was going to insult Robottom. The fish was still very hot as it had just come out of the black sizzling skillet… the thin cornbread acted as insulation from the scorching hot fish. I thought about my options and wondered what to do. Instincts took over, I thought about what my mom would want me to do, and I devoured the fish and cornbread. I thought that I would wretch as it slid down my throat, but surprisingly it was quite good. As Robottom said, it wasn't New Orleans cuisine, but it was the best that the "batture" had to offer at the moment.

"Through the indiscriminate, uneven flames, the smoke, and amber and yellow flying embers tossed by the fire, I could see that Robottom was also relishing every bit of the fish he had prepared and in between bites he would chuckle as he thought about the situation "we" were in and the "conversation" we were having. Robottom chewed with his mouth open and tried to talk, even with his mouth full of fish and cornbread, resulting from time to time, in an eruption of fried fish and cornbread raining down in every direction. He was a crude old man, but the sight of him relishing his meal that he was selflessly sharing with me, allowed me to relax for the first time since I started this ill-fated, insane adventure. I felt a slight smile appear suddenly and for the first time since hearing the jeers of my friends as this misadventure began, I felt safe.

Small pieces of fish and cornmeal sat precariously on his white shaggy mustache and beard ready to tumble into obscurity in the white sands of the batture. As he chewed, his lips moved up and down like pistons and pushed his massive nose up and down with each bite. At a different time, and different place, I am sure it would have been comical, but tonight, it struck me as just the quirky mannerism of a very nice colored man who enjoyed and made the most of his simple, uncomplicated life even in this unlikeliest of settings.

"So ya 20..., huh?" he said again as he laughed at my obvious lie. "The Book say I gots ta love my neighbor and the Book say I gots ta love my enemy, but the Book don't say I gots ta love a liar." His smile covered his face as he continued laughing. "I got boogas older en you boy…

"You got a name," Robottom asked.

"Yes sir, I'm Paul Manz," I answered.

"Paul Manz," he repeated.

"Boy, you getting' warm?" he asked.

Mumbling, I said, "Yeah, I'm much warmer, but I think you broke my shoulder."

I broke ya shoulda? I broke ya shoulda, Robottom screamed.

“Yeah…”’ I said.

“He paused, hands on his knees, peering at me through the firelight.

“Boy, I’m sixty-five years olda den you,” he said, shaking his head. “I think it’s yessa…”

“Yes sir, I immediately responded, “I think you broke my shoulder.”

“Robottom still sitting on “his side” of the fire, continued to enjoy every mouthful of the catfish he had just fried as if it were a filet at Antoine’s. I only had one eye open. I squinted due to the glare of the fire and because my eyes had been exposed to the nasty, brown water of the river they stung and prevented me from focusing on anything……… except that for some reason, I was totally focused on everything this old man was doing, and I hung on everything he had to say. I had one eye closed and was squinting out of the other but seemed to be seeing more clearly than I had ever seen anything in my life.

“One eye was all that was needed as all I saw was a man who was totally content with his station in life. I knew nothing about him, except that he had saved my life, he was kind and thoughtful and he enjoyed the simple things… like his river catfish. Robottom told me that while fishing for catfish in the river, he had seen my raised arm traveling down the river propelled by the rapid current. He had failed several times to fish me out of the muddy water and told me that he had to run downstream and had to climb out on an old willow tree branch to get to a point where he could pull me out of the current. I was exhausted but not so tired that I didn’t realize that he had placed his life in jeopardy by doing that.

After several minutes of enjoying his meal, Robottom said, “Boy, I’m no smart man. I ain’t no stupid man neither. I do love ma Lord and all ma life I served my Lord working and preachin’ up and down dis big river and on them boats that travel on it.

Robottom used that same thin willow branch that he had used to cook with, to point towards the river as if it gave accent to what he was saying. "I got a roof over my head and as long as that river has water in it, I'll have food to eat.

He stood and reached across the blazing fire to hand me another piece of river catfish wrapped in cornbread. He handed it to me with the same tenderness he used when he'd bandaged my bleeding hand. And again, without a second thought, I accepted. I bit into it. It was hot—still sizzling from the pan—but it was good.

I chewed slowly, my busted ribs flaring up with every breath, but for the first time since diving into that cursed current, I wasn't thinking about pain. I wasn't thinking about the cold. I wasn't thinking about the river, or Bebe, or my busted-up shoulder. I was just sitting by a fire, wrapped in a stranger's coat, eating something warm that tasted like something prepared at home even if it wasn't.

And in that strange, quiet moment, surrounded by smoke and sparks and the wind whispering through the trees, I felt a kind of warmth—not just from the fire, but deep down. In my bones. In my soul. As I ate my fish and corn bread and although still in intense pain, I found myself oddly relishing the moment.

We hadn't spoken in several minutes. The crackling fire filled the silence. I had just about finished the last of the fish Robottom gave me, still feeling the sting in my ribs and the heaviness in my shoulder, when I muttered, more to myself than anything—

"I swam across," I offered reluctantly.

"Robottom screamed, "Ya what?"

"I swam across the river," I repeated a little louder. I'm from Ama.

"Why would ya do somethin' so dumb?

"Boy, you look normal but I don't know, maybe I should throw ya nekkit butt back in the river…" he threatened?

"You just jumped in and decided you would swim the Miss'ippi River?" he questioned.

"What would be in a boy's head that would make him do such a thing?" he asked?

"And, boy, tell me, (as he paused to attack another piece of catfish) what plans had you made once ya' made it ta this side of the river," he asked as he once again, sprayed catfish and cornbread in all directions in this cool, September night.

"What plans, I asked"?

"Well, did ya' plan on walkin' into a stor' and buyin' some new britches since ya got here without any? "Or, he shouted, "Since ya' nekkit as a jay bird, were ya' plannin' to swim BACK ACROSS dat river?" he asked sarcastically.

"The way Dad said it—his voice climbing, made everyone listening in that principal's office burst into laughter. Even the secretaries couldn't help but smile.

It was a rare kind of laughter—relieved, cathartic. The tension had been building for so long during Dad's story, that now every jab from Robottom felt like a gift, a release.

"Boy," he said, softening a bit...Paul.... this was the first time he'd used my name. "You just a young, silly boy...I know, I know. I was "20" once," Robottom laughed out loud at the thought. A mouthful of half-eaten catfish and cornmeal hung in the mist.

I was still curled up lying near the fire, eyes half closed, trying not to breathe too hard. Every breath was a reminder of what I'd done to myself. The pain in my ribs flared each time I shifted, but I couldn't stop watching Robottom. The way the light of the fire flickered on his face, the way he sat so calmly and comfortably as if he'd been living by that riverbank for a hundred years.

"I don't know nothin' 'bout ya' boy, but ya didn't get across dat ribba by yoself...," he remarked.

"I didn't quite understand what Robottom meant when he said that I hadn't crossed the river by myself. I watched him across the fire as the shadow of the flame danced on his face and as I waited anxiously for more of an explanation of what he meant.

"Brother," he began again, quieter now, his voice changed...there was something deeper in it... something heavier. "I have worked on boats all up and down the Miss'ippi and I has know'd people, plenty young, strong men dat worked on dat river fa years and dat in one instant of a second took one wrong step, one slip, a lost grip on a rope, a slip on a frozen deck, a trip over a mooring line, men dat fall into this river and never come up. I seen men fall into that muddy, nasty water yelling and screaming like a newborn. I seen the eyes of some of the best men I have ever know'd ...wide…scared…worse than scared 'cause dey know dey staring death in the face and it no longa if, but when they gonna die… All those men who never went home to their woman and young uns, every one of them…would love to have had one mo' chance. One mo' step to get into that boat… but they got nothin' but another mouth full of the muddiest, nastiest water. And boy, I think about those big eyes... I think about those arms reachin…' reachin'… hands searching for anything that would get them outta that water...fingers beggin' for somethin' to grasp... and with hands completely empty but lungs completely full of water, they was nothin' left. And then I think about you… swimming across the Miss'ippi River... Lordy, Lordy, Lordy."

"God gave ya something special tonight boy and you don't even see it. God gave you a life back. He must love ya. He must have a special plan fa' you because good, strong, men have fallen into dat ribba and many men never come out of that muddy water alive," he insisted… "Na da Lord says ya reaps what ya sow and if ya believe dat, and I do, then ya shoulda never come outta that nasty river and ya shouldn't a be sitting here in front of my fire." You is a lucky little boy, he barked.

"Ya' don't know how lucky ya is….as this river is a nasty monsta," he insisted.

"Boy, don't you ever forget, the Lord has something special in store for you. All of the things I have been through for the past 70 plus years happened so I'd be by this riverbank fishin' so that I could pull you out. We ain't met by accident. This was meant to be. The Lord got something special fo' ya boy." The Lord gots somethin' special fo' ya," he repeated.

"Eat dis, boy." "Dats good river catfish." Careful na, der may be bones in dat fish."

"Robottom handed me another big chunk of fried catfish along with a thin piece of cornbread….and cautioned me about how hot it was and cautioned against getting a fish bone caught in my throat." After eating several pieces of fish, I thought, now you caution me about bones. Fish bones… another reason I had never eaten fish.

"After crossing the river dats the last thing we needed….," he joked.

Robottom said, "If it wasn't fo' fish I suspect I'd die."

"I thanked Mr. Robottom, told him that I enjoyed the fish and told him again that I had never had fish before, 'cause my mom didn't like the way it smelled."

"Robottom stared at the glowing embers in the fire as he scribbled in the bone-dry, sandy soil with his same, thin willow twig when the silence of the night was shattered by the sound of a ship moving along the river headed upriver towards Baton Rouge.

"Booonnncccckkkk, Booonnncccckkkk," screamed the ship's horn as it headed to its northerly destination. The ear-splitting sound of the ship's horn brought back recent memories of my nerve-wracking experience on the river and dredged up unpleasant memories that I hoped I would be able to put behind me, in time. The pounding noise of the ship's engine added insult to injury and made me relive very unpleasant memories of my time in the muddy waters of the river.

"The pan that he had used to fry his fish, and his quick bread was totally empty now as every wonderful bite had been eaten. With our "meal" over, I wanted to ask him questions about his life but felt like I would have been prying. Was he or had he ever been married? Did he have children? What kind of work did he do on the river? Was the batture really his home?

"I was still lying on my right side curled up like a baby trying to stay as still as possible as even the slightest movement was excruciatingly painful, both in my ribs and my shoulder. My right hand was my pillow, and I was looking at Robottom through the glow of the fire. The flames were now as high as they had ever been as the strong, wind continued to blow off the river, whipping through the batture. Embers and sparks continued to swirl as they were tossed in the air by the strong, westerly winds that were coming off the river. I had never noticed how the light danced, and how beautiful it really was. It was getting more and more difficult to discern Robottom's facial features in the darkness that had enveloped us both. Robottom said, Yo momma gonna be happy to see you tomorra" and he asked me if I wanted something else to drink."

No, sir, please. I've never had wine before..."

"You still hasn't, he interrupted as he laughed and laughed as he rocked back and forth, slapping his knee. He was right as I had quickly dispensed of the one mouthful I had been given earlier, into the sandy soil of the batture."

"And I think I've had enough water for one day," I continued.

"Robottom leaned behind himself, picked up another piece of driftwood and threw it onto the fire. Bright red, yellow and orange embers flew up and out in every direction and I watched as they danced in the darkness that surrounded me and Robottom. Me and the guys spent many summer nights under the stars and around a campfire, but I had never noticed how beautiful a fire could be. As I said, even with only one eye open, it was as if I was seeing things I had never seen before. The night was pitch black dark and except for the wind pushing through the thin limbs of the willow trees and the sounds of the river, it was a quiet, peaceful setting. Apparently, there wasn't much along this stretch of the east bank of the river... wherever I was."

"After several minutes and I don't know why, I broke the silence by declaring, "14."

"Whas sat boy," Robottom asked?

"14... I'm fourteen years old." I said.

"14 years old," he shouted. "My boots is older than that, boy," he laughed.

"Robottom told me to put my head down and rest and that he'd see me here in the morning. He reassured me by telling me that we'd find my mom and dad in the morning."

"Mom and dad… Those words hung in the air like Robottom's catfish and cornbread showers that had filled the cool, evening air just moments ago. I wasn't certain if I should tell him about Dad. I wanted desperately to see my mom tomorrow, but also would have given just about everything I owned to see my dad tomorrow as well. I was not in a good frame of mind because of all that had transpired today. I was guilt ridden and my every thought was the recurring idea that I had caused my mom to worry, but when Mr. Robottom mentioned my dad, my eyes welled up with tears. It hadn't been that long that Dad had left us, and the trauma of his death was still felt all these months later. I missed my daddy desperately.

"In that quiet setting, I thought of my dad at Providence and the times we had working together to keep Mr. Sanders machines, trucks and tractors running with J.W. Robert. I missed Dad and I didn't even have a chance to say good-bye. I thought of him daily. How could I not. I worked at the same place he worked. I used the same tools he had used and in some cases tools he had made. I did the things that he had taught me to do. I had tried to put his memory away in a special vault in my mind that kept the memories safely secured inside and the threat of pain and the insecurity... completely and forever locked up… locked. I didn't know if I should share any of this with Mr. Robottom. What good would it do to dredge up memories that I had expended so much time, effort and energy to keep buried.

"I would suspect your daddy is on this river right now looking for your nekkit little butt," Mr. Robottom offered.

"My dad isn't looking for me," I said with a certain anger that was palpable and very inappropriate. Why would I lash out at Mr.

Robottom when he had nothing to do with anything that had occurred in my life prior to just an hour or two ago.

"Sho he is, Paul," Mr Robottom countered. "If ya were my son, I'd be out here..."

"My dad isn't living," I interrupted.

"What you say, son?" Mr. Robottom said quietly, almost tenderly. I saw Mr. Robottom's ruffled brow out of my one eye in the mist and darkness that was encircling Mr. Robottom as the fire continued to roar. As he stared at me with his wide eyes in anticipation of the answer to his question, his head was cocked to one side as he waited anxiously for my response."

"My father died on Feb. 7th," I said.

"Paul," is all he said. It was all he needed to say. There was a long pause as Mr. Robottom made use of the willow branch to continue sketching in the sands of the batture. I wondered what masterpiece he was creating. I wondered what he was thinking.

"Boy that's terrible. I'm sorry. I'm sorry I even brought it up. How sad for ya. Mr. Robottom said quietly, softly, slowly as if he was measuring every word for its appropriateness. He was now staring at me as he took his massive hand and stroked his shabby gray beard. I could tell he was uncomfortable.

"My dad worked at Providence Plantation in Ama." I continued. "He worked on tractors and the equipment Mr. Sanders used in makin' sugar. There was a terrible accident one day and my dad died trying to prevent others from being hurt. I don't know exactly what happened to my dad as no one has ever told me... won't tell me... Whatever happened, it must have been bad. My dad left early that morning to head to Providence and I remember waving goodbye as he turned onto the River Road in his old Ford pickup, just as he had for so many mornings. This morning was different. It was the last time I ever saw him."

"I'm sorry, Paul. "No young un should have to go through somethin' like dat. You's all yo' momma got. You got no business in the river. She must be having a fit tonight."

There was silence for several minutes and as I looked at Mr. Robottom, framed in the blackness of the batture, I realized how strange all of this was. The silly mistake I made trying to prove that I was something that I was not, a mistake that almost killed me, had brought together two men of extremely diverse backgrounds and we seemed to have bonded in the short time we had been together. I thought it strange that a fire separated us here on the batture and the color of our skin would have separated us away from the batture, but gazing at Robottom through the prism of a single eye and through the now intense flames of the fire allowed me to continue seeing things clearer that I had ever seen them before. An elderly wise colored man and a young, immature white kid had nothing in common except that we seemed to have bonded by the unlikeliest of circumstances and by a surprisingly satisfying banquet of river catfish and cornbread as well as friendly conversation. The man sitting in front of me was someone I could never forget, and I was so anxious for my mom to meet him.

"I am tired, and that fire feels good. Thank you, Mr. Robottom."

Robottom just tipped his head stroked his beard again with his massive fingers and simply smiled a toothless smile. I thought about tomorrow and the grand reunion and I thought about how happy I would be to see my mom and how much I wanted to introduce her to Robottom who was now humming as he played in the embers of the now dying fire. I recognized he was humming a hymn that I knew well as we often sang it at Holy Rosary…

It took a moment, but I remembered the song and some of the words:

Standing on the promises of Christ my King,
Through eternal ages let His praises ring,
Glory in the highest, I will shout and sing,
Standing on the promises of God.

Standing, standing,
Standing on the promises of God my Savior;
Standing, standing,
I'm standing on the promises of God.

"I was exhausted. I hurt worse than I ever had hurt before and, though I didn't want to, I began to think about how foolish and thoughtless I had been. In many ways, that pain was much worse than the pain I felt from my shoulder and ribs. My mom had been through so much with the death of my father. She had had a difficult time not only because of his death but the horrible nature of the accident and the uncertainties with losing the family's breadwinner. The little money I made wasn't much. Mr. Sanders gave me a fair wage for what I did, and it covered the basics but just barely. How could I have been so thoughtless to put all that in jeopardy? What would have happened to my mom? Who would have cared for her? My thoughtless act had put everything in jeopardy. As I said, I was seeing things with a clarity I had never seen before."

"I desperately wished that there was some way that I could contact my mom to assure her that I was okay... or at least what was left of me was okay. Even if I could have contacted her, I wouldn't have any idea of how to tell her where I was. Other than being on the batture next to the river, I hadn't a clue if I was close to New Orleans, in Chalmette or in any of the other small river towns that surrounded the Crescent City.

I wondered what she was doing at this moment.

How upset was she?

Would she be able to find a way to forgive me? She had rarely been upset with me.

Would she forgive my stupidity...my thoughtlessness?

What did she have for supper?

How would I find my way out of the batture?

What would I do for clothes?

In which direction should I walk to find a way to contact people.

How would Robottom help me? What a mess.

Weary but thankfully, sleep came quickly as Robottom continued to hum that "familiar" hymn.

Mr. Robottom

CHAPTER 7

I'M FOUND

"Boys, here is where the story gets really strange," my dad said, leaning forward now, his voice quieter, more deliberate. You could hear a pin drop in that office.

"The next morning, I woke up when I heard a man yelling. It was a voice that cut straight through the fog of my pain and confusion.

'Sheriff Triche! Sheriff! Ova heya… ova heya! Is he dead, Sheriff? Boys, ova here. We got him!'

"It took me a second to realize what I was hearing wasn't part of a dream. I had been drifting in and out of a shallow, painful sleep, still curled up in the sand where Robottom had left me beside the dying fire. The morning sun was brutal—sharp and white and far too bright. I could only manage to open one eye, and even that felt like too much.

Kneeling right in front of me was a man in uniform. A deputy. His face was drawn with concern.

'Son, what's your name?' he asked gently.

I could barely get it out. 'Paul,' I whispered.

'Sheriff! Sheriff!' he yelled louder this time. 'Ova heya… we got Paul Manz!'

Suddenly, I heard boots as deputies were running in my direction. Another figure stepped into view—older, heavier, with a commanding presence that silenced the chaos.

It was Sheriff Joseph Triche—the sheriff of Jefferson Parish, who approached cautiously and when he saw me lying naked, bloodied, and shaking in the sand, he stepped back, yanked off his own jacket, and barked orders like a man possessed.

'Good Lord, Deputy—wrap this around that poor boy!' 'Yell at Leon and get my car here right now! I'll meet you at the top of the levee—NOW!'

The deputy bent over me and peeled back the stiff, piece of cardboard someone had laid across my lower body. He draped the sheriff's coat over me like a blanket. I cried out involuntarily when he touched me. My whole body screamed. The ribs, the shoulder, every breath felt like a knife to the chest.

The deputy froze, startled at my reaction as any movement of my upper body sent sharp pains throughout my body. 'What's wrong, son?' the sheriff asked again, now crouching beside me.

'Shoulder… and my chest,' was all I could say to the Sheriff as that was all I could get out. I was so tired, so cold, in such pain and still so confused.

I… I need you to find Mr. Robottom and the sheriff asked me who Mr. Robottom was.

'Robottom?' the deputy asked, confused. 'Who's Robottom?'

I tried to lift my head. Slowly. Painfully. I looked around with my one good eye. All I could see were the legs of lawmen standing over me—shiny boots, stiff trousers, badges. But no Robottom. No battered coat. No skillet. No fire.

'He's the man who pulled me from the river,' I said, more urgently now. 'He carried me here… made this fire… wrapped this cloth around my hand, gave me his jacket.' I tried to raise my hand, to show the bloodied cloth that had been wrapped around it, but there was nothing there. My hand was bare, raw, crusted with dried blood. The cloth was gone.

'An old colored man named Robottom,' I added, trying to sound sure even though I was starting to feel unsure of everything.

The sheriff squinted. 'Son, I've walked every inch of this batture for the last several miles. There's not a colored man anywhere around here—except for a few good men who came from Ama to help us search for you.'

'Where's the fire?' another deputy asked, looking around.

'Right there,' I said, pointing weakly to the spot where Robottom's fire had burned brightly just hours ago. 'Right where you're standing.'

But there was nothing. No fire. No ashes. No blackened pan. No signs of anyone ever being there.

I could feel it—everyone around me thought I was delusional, or worse, lying. I looked down at my bare, filthy hand and felt a sudden surge of panic. Had it all been a dream? Had Robottom even existed?

But I knew what I saw. I knew what I felt. Robottom had been real. He had saved my life.

And now… he was gone.

"I was totally confused and said firmly, "Robottom pulled me from the river and hurt my shoulder when he threw me on the ground. He gave me his jacket, he cleaned me up, he gave me some wine to drink and fish to eat that he cooked himself," I added.

"He gave you wine to drink?" someone from the crowd asked in disbelief, the words slicing through the morning air like a whip. There was a sudden murmur that rippled through the deputies, and another voice jumped in, louder this time. "Is he drunk, sir? He's drunk, isn't he? Damned fool kids," the deputy muttered, his judgment sharp and full of frustration. "The kid's been drinking."

But before the words could settle or anyone else could pile on, Sheriff Triche turned to face the man with a look so cold, so firm, it could've stopped a train in its tracks and the deputy understood it was time to calm down. It wasn't loud. It didn't need to be. The message in the sheriff's eyes was louder than any outburst. The deputy shrank back a step, immediately understanding that he'd overstepped and it was time to keep quiet.

Then the sheriff turned his attention back to me, this naked, busted-up boy lying in the sand, and bellowed again, "Where is Leon and my car?" He shook his head and muttered something under his breath, then looked down at me again, his voice gentler now. "Son, there is no one here named Robottom. You weren't wearing any jacket when we found you, and there's no fire around here. Look at this place. This parish hasn't had a drop of rain since May. Every blade of grass, every weed, every stick of driftwood on this side of the levee is bone dry. If someone had lit a fire down here, we'd have seen it from New Orleans, and all we'd be finding this morning is your scorched behind."

He knelt down beside me as gently as he could. "There's no fire, son," he said again, softer this time. "There's nothing wrapped around your hand. And again, no jacket."

"But sir," I croaked, my voice barely louder than a whisper, "the fire was here. Right here in front of me. Robottom gave me fish and put his jacket on me."

The sheriff offered a quiet smile, not mocking, not cruel—just a tired, compassionate smile from a man who'd seen too much. "Son, the only thing you had on when we found you was a dirty old piece of cardboard."

I didn't know what to say. My head was spinning. The sheriff's words were spinning. My whole body ached, not just from the busted ribs or the throbbing shoulder but from the fog that was overtaking my mind. Was last night even real? Had I dreamed the fire, the fish, the coat, the kindness of a strange man on the riverbank? If Mr. Robottom wasn't real, how did I get out of the river?

"Boys, yell to the men in the boats," the sheriff ordered over his shoulder. "Tell 'em we found the Manz kid. They can turn around and head back upriver. Meet us at the ferry landing."

He kept barking instructions like a conductor in front of an exhausted, makeshift orchestra. "Barnabas, head across the river. Tell the other crew we've got the boy. Deputy Lorio, drive to the ferry landing and get it across to the West Bank now. The sheriff and the boy's mother are there. Tell them he's alive, banged up but alive. We're taking him straight to the hospital in St. Rose."

I don't remember much after that.

I've been told later that the moment Sheriff Triche bent down to scoop me up, and the pain from my ribs and shoulder shot through me so sharply that I blacked out right there on the batture. One second, I was staring at the legs of the deputies standing over me, the next second—nothing. I passed out cold.

They said the sheriff himself carried me up the levee and placed me into his car. Said he drove the whole way himself, not trusting anyone else to do it. But I don't remember a single bump in the road, a single street sign, a single turn of the tires.

While I was being driven to St. Rose, the rest of the rescue effort was still in motion. Deputy Lorio did exactly what he was told. The ferry—our old George Prince—was just arriving from the West Bank, with only two cars on board. They rolled off and, without picking up the others waiting on the East Bank, the ferry turned right around. No hesitation. The blaring horn of the George Prince shattered the sleepy quiet of the river as it headed back to the West Bank carrying the deputy and the good news that I had been found.

They said the horn didn't stop the whole way across. Just blasted, long and steady, a beacon of hope cutting through the uncertainty and fear of the moment. Back at the Ferry Inn—a run-down little building at the top of the levee on the west bank of the river—the small crowd that had kept vigil through the night stirred at the sound. Sheriff Vicknair and my mom were both inside, sitting in silence and dread when the horn began. Someone ran in shouting, "They found him! Sheriff, they found the boy!"

I learned later that Sheriff Vicknair, sheriff of St. Charles Parish and my mom had been waiting at the Ferry Inn, a tiny run-down restaurant at the top of the levee on the West Bank by the ferry landing when they were disturbed by the distinctive blaring of the George Prince's horn. Again, they blew that horn the entire 1200 feet across the river and before it had arrived someone flew into the Ferry inn and yelled, “They found him, Sheriff!” they tell me my mom almost collapsed right there and was steadied by the well-wishers who had gathered with her. The vigil at the Ferry Inn had been a long one as most folks gathered had already assumed the worst and were trying to prepare themselves for the inevitable bad news that they knew would come sometime later today. Mr. Vitrano had kept his little restaurant open all night and had coffee and beignets ready for anyone who needed comfort, for anyone who’d come to wait, hope and mourn, ...if they had to.

But now, thanks to God and a man no one could find, there was something better than mourning.

Sheriff Vicknair and my mom began the slow walk down the levee toward the ferry landing just as the George Prince was approaching. The sheriff walked steady and upright beside her, but I know every step she took felt like a mile. My mom had been told I was found, but not in what condition? She didn’t know if the boy waiting across that river was her son—or just her son’s body.

After losing my father earlier that summer, I can’t begin to imagine what that 50-yard walk from the Ferry Inn to the rusted, time-worn landing must have felt like. I’m convinced it was the second longest walk of her life—second only to the one she made the day she buried her husband. And now here she was, praying that this morning wouldn’t end with another loss.

As the George Prince crept closer to the shore, the wind whipping off the river carried voices ahead of it. Deputy Lorio stood on the bow, waving wildly and yelling above the churning engines. His voice cracked under the strain, but he shouted with everything he had.

“They found Paul!” he called out. “He’s banged up, but he’s alive!”

The words struck the crowd like a bolt of lightning. Cheers erupted. Someone cried out in praise. But for my mom, it was too much. Her knees gave way beneath her, and she collapsed right there at the edge of the levee, crying uncontrollably. It was a cry of grief, yes, but also of overwhelming relief. The people around her—friends, neighbors, strangers—rushed to lift her up, wrapping their arms around her, supporting her, steadying her. They cried too.

That vigil at the Ferry Inn had gone on through the entire night, and by dawn, nearly a hundred people had come and gone, many of them staying even when they feared the worst. They had braced themselves for the kind of news nobody wanted to hear. But now, against all odds, it was good news. It was a miracle. I was alive.

Deputy Lorio regained his composure and stepped off the ferry to address the crowd. He told them I was being taken to St. Rose Hospital, and the George Prince was to take the sheriff, my mom, and anyone else who wanted to come over immediately to the Destrehan landing. A parade of cars, rumbled onto the deck of the old ferry. And as she pulled away from the bank, loaded down with joyful passengers, I'd bet the George Prince never made a happier crossing in all her years on the river.

Six hours. That's how long I'd been in the river—tossed, swallowed, almost claimed for good. Six hours of fear, exhaustion, and desperation. The George Prince crossed that same water in six minutes. It's a humbling thing when you realize how much life can change in the span of a single river crossing.

I was told later that I'd been pulled from the river just north of Harahan, Louisiana. Somehow, I had traveled twenty-three miles down the Mississippi. And I had been right, it turns out. The bend in the river just before Harahan—where the water curves sharply to the right—was what had ultimately saved me. The current had pushed me toward the east bank and delivered me into the hands of a stranger I'd never forget. The strong westerly winds that had blown all afternoon and evening also helped to push me to the east bank of the river.

My mom arrived at the hospital after I'd already fallen asleep. I didn't see her at first, but when I woke up a short time after her arrival, our reunion was everything I had longed for. She was by my side, eyes red and swollen from crying, her face lined with exhaustion and love. She didn't scold me. She didn't yell. She just sat there holding my hand, and I cried. I cried harder than I ever had before—not from the pain in my ribs or my busted shoulder, but from the deeper pain in my heart. I had hurt her. I had terrified her. I had nearly left her alone in this world. And I would never forgive myself for that.

When I finally told her how sorry I was, how I had tried to turn back after just a short distance from the west bank, she listened. Quietly. Patiently. After a long moment, she looked at me with tears running down her cheeks and said, "I knew you were going to be found. I knew you were going to be okay."

Then she smiled faintly and added, "Your daddy always told me it took him months to teach you the difference between a wrench and a pair of pliers. He said the good Lord wouldn't put in all that effort just to take you away from me now."

I laughed at that. Just a small chuckle. Then my ribs reminded me exactly how badly they were broken, and the laugh turned into a painful groan.

I was still in rough shape and had to rest for a couple of days. But eventually, I had to face Sheriff Vicknair and tell him everything. He sat across from me, solemn and understanding, and filled in the blanks from his side. He told me that when I was swept away so quickly by the current, the boys I had been with didn't hesitate. They ran straight to Providence Plantation and told Mr. Sanders. From there, the word spread like wildfire. Parents were called. A caravan of cars and pickups rushed off to Hahnville to notify the sheriff while others ran to the riverbank, desperate to help.

They didn't know if I had made it out alive. But they were going to look until they found me—or until they couldn't look anymore.

And somehow, by the grace of God, they did.

Other men headed downriver and parked their pickups along the levee, stepping out and standing silently on the top of the levee, peering down into the shadowy waters of the Mississippi. The sun had dipped behind the towering, green embankment on the West Bank, casting long, slanted shadows across the face of the river. It was quiet. Too quiet. The kind of quiet that makes your stomach turn. With the river's surface so dark and restless, the men strained their eyes against the fading light, hoping—no, praying—to catch a glimpse of anything. A ripple. A bobbing piece of driftwood. A hand. Anything.

But the river wasn't talking.

It didn't take long for the last sliver of sunlight to disappear. A heavy curtain of darkness dropped over the water like a closing stage curtain, swallowing up the hopes of the watchers in an inky shroud. Once it was dark, there was nothing left to do but wait. Eyes can't search where there is no light.

But even as the night set in, the effort didn't wane.

Before sunrise, the entire community—Ama, Luling, Hahnville, and even folks from down the River Road—had already begun to gather at the ferry landing. They didn't need instructions. They didn't need a reason. They just came. It's how small towns work. When something happens to one of their own, everyone shows up. They were ready at first light with torches, boots, and blankets, prepared to walk every step of that batture, all the way to New Orleans if they had to.

Word had already spread through every church, café, barbershop, and gas station. People came out in trucks, on horseback and in weather-worn wagons, some still in their church clothes from the night before, others wearing work boots and mud-stained jeans. They didn't know what they were going to find—or if they were going to find anything at all—but they knew they weren't going to stop looking.

Sheriff Vicknair was already organizing crews for both banks of the river, working through the night and ready to deploy at first light. It wasn't hard to find volunteers on the east bank of the river. All it took was one phone call to the Jefferson Parish Sheriff's Office and help was already on the way. Within the hour, several search teams had rolled out, heading upriver to the St. Charles–Jefferson Parish line, just like the sheriff suggested. They joined the local crews, led by Sheriff Triche himself.

That East Bank team would be the one to find me.

By dawn, the river was lined with boats, their oars dipping into the brown muddy waters of the river and knocking loudly and continuously against the sides of the wooden skiffs …. echoing off of the levees. The men inside them were dragging their eyes along both the water's surface and the muddy shoreline. They searched everything. Every floating log, every tangled tree limb that touched the water's edge. They stopped at sandbars and picked through piles of driftwood, one branch at a time. Every pile of rocks, every abandoned tire, every broken tree trunk—they checked them all. The river had a way of holding things, and they weren't going to miss a single sign.

The batture was being combed inch by inch.

The sun climbed higher, blazing across a cloudless blue sky. The temperature rose. So did the tension. By mid-morning, the crews had covered several miles, their boots caked in wet sand, their shirts soaked with sweat.

It was around that time—mid-morning, maybe a little later—that one of the deputies caught sight of something peculiar. A piece of cardboard. Nothing unusual, not on the batture. But it was sticking up at a strange angle, half-buried in the sand. The deputy was told, "Go kick that thing and move it out of the way."

He jogged over casually and gave it a boot.

The cardboard screamed.

The deputy staggered back in shock, nearly falling over me. Under that piece of cardboard was a mangled, shivering, bloodied teenager.

It was me.

That's how they found me.

"Guys," I said, glancing around at the wide-eyed crowd gathered in that school office, I never found out what happened to Mr.

Robottom. The thought of never seeing Robottom again saddened me. I didn't really care if people believed me or not, but I deeply cared that I would never be able to thank Mr. Robottom for saving my life. I was appreciative of his tender care and felt a deep, profound sadness when I finally came to terms that I would never be able to thank him for pulling me out of the river and saving my hide. I was respectful to everyone that asked about that night, and I tried not to be rude to anyone when they insisted that none of the things that I knew I had experienced, had happened. After some time, I stopped telling the story. I stopped trying to convince people that what I had shared was true, but I never stopped believing it.

While I was recovering, I had several visits from Sheriff Vicknair. He came by to talk, mostly. But he also had questions. He wanted to know how the whole thing had started. What had possessed me to try such a thing? And more importantly—what had happened when I reached the other side?

I told him everything. Everything I told you.

I didn't change a word.

And here is the strangest part of this story. I also told the doctors that the inside of my jaw was very painful. Thinking that I may have cracked or loosened a tooth when I got jammed by that submerged log in the river, the doctors looked in my mouth to try to find out the cause of the pain. What they found was life changing…………… Boys and girls, the doctors found only one thing in my mouth……..stuck in one cheek and it was the source of all the pain I was experiencing…

"At this point, Dad stopped talking and reached for his wallet. All of us looked at each other as we could not image what had been found. The doorway to the office was now packed with football players and several coeds who had been at cheer practice. They were all focused with an intensity not often seen in a high school by young people who did not necessarily possess a lengthy attention span. Students voluntarily hurried in the office that just moments before would have been avoided at all costs.

"Dad reminded us that up until the night he had met Robottom—who, as everyone insisted, didn't exist—he had never eaten fish. As strange as that sounds for a boy raised in South Louisiana, it was true. The catfish that Robottom had cooked in that blackened iron skillet over an open fire, the fish he had prepared with such care, wrapped in a thin piece of cornbread and shared so generously… was the very first fish Dad had ever tasted. The very first fish he had ever eaten.

"Dad unfolded the aged piece of parchment slowly, delicately, with the kind of reverence one gives to something sacred. The paper was yellowed, stained, and frayed along the edges—creased and cracked in a dozen places. It had clearly been opened and folded again countless times. It had lived for decades in the safe pocket of his worn brown wallet. Every eye in the crowded school office was on his hands.

"My dad opened his billfold and slowly, very carefully took out that yellow, stained, frayed around the edges, piece of parchment. It was obvious from the condition of the paper that it had been opened and refolded many times over the years and had a permanent home in my dad's wallet. He slowly unfolded the parchment. Every eye in the place was on my dad's hands. The secretaries stood so that they could see what was in the parchment. Mr. Labry did not move as it appeared that he had heard this story a time or two and knew what to expect. The entire football team was leaning over my dad's massive khaki covered shoulders. Several other students were now peering through the massive glass window that separated the outer office from the hallway. Several parents now had joined the crowd, as well as the driver of the transfer bus.

"And then, in a voice low and solemn, Dad said, 'That morning, after the most horrifying night of my life, the doctors found this.' He opened his palm, revealing the small, brittle thing resting in the paper. 'It was lodged in my cheek—this tiny thing causing the soreness in my jaw. This is it. Right here. This was the pain.' He paused, lifting the delicate object between his fingers. 'A fish bone.'

"There were audible gasps in the office. And for those who had been quietly doubting, this was the moment that turned skepticism into awe. It's a fish bone. From the catfish Robottom caught that night. The catfish he cooked for me. The one I ate by that fire on the batture.' The weight of his voice, the conviction in his words—it was impossible not to believe. Whether anyone thought Robottom had truly been there or not, it didn't matter. Because for Dad, it had happened. He had lived it. And the tiny bone in his wallet was proof enough.

"The story ended. But the silence in the room lingered like smoke after a fire. No one moved. No one dared break the moment. And I—I was stunned. I had never been prouder of my father. Never. Not because he had survived the river, or because he had shared a story with such humor, heart and conviction, but because in that moment, standing in front of a room full of students, teachers, and strangers, he let us see something we rarely saw—his vulnerability, his faith, and the extraordinary compassion of a man named Robottom, who might have been real, or might have been something more.

"As the crowd began to drift out and the school day came back into focus, Mr. Labry took the floor with his usual sense of purpose. He reminded us of what the story had really been about—foolish pride, second chances, the fragility of life, and the grace that sometimes finds us in our worst hour. But even his well-intentioned moral felt like a shadow after the light my father had brought into that room.

"Later, as we walked out together toward Dad's pickup, he veered toward the row of massive live oaks that lined the walkways like sentinels. Without a word, he motioned me to follow. We sat beneath one of those massive trees, its roots pushing up through the earth like the veins of the past, reminding us of things long buried but never gone.

"I was unsure of what was coming. I braced myself. But Dad just smiled and said, 'Did you swing first?'

"'Sir?' I asked.

"'The fight. Did you start it?'

"'No sir, I didn't,' I said quickly. 'Bebe Troxclair's two feet taller than me, Dad. I'm dumb, but I ain't that dumb.'

"'Well?' he prompted, and I told him everything. How Bebe knocked my books down, kicked them into the gravel parking area, how he shoved me against the gym wall, how I punched him out of sheer anger and frustration. How I got clobbered and saw stars before Mr. Williams pulled us apart.

"Dad didn't interrupt. He just watched me closely, eyes squinting in that familiar way that made you feel both nervous and safe. When I was done, I braced for a lecture.

"But instead, the corners of his mouth curled into a grin, and then he threw his head back and laughed. Really laughed. He pulled me into a hug—tight, warm, full of pride. 'Mattie,' he said, 'I don't ever want you to start a fight. But Mr. Williams already told us what happened. I knew you didn't start that fight. Because I know how big Bebe Troxclair is. And I knew you aren't that dumb.'

"He laughed again and playfully shoved me into the tall grass like we were just two boys sharing a secret under the big oak tree. It was a moment I'll never forget. A moment that made me feel like no matter how strange or terrifying life gets, I'd always have Dad—and that was enough.

"And that's our story.

My dad's. And mine."

The End.

www.ingramcontent.com/pod-product-compliance
Lightning Source LLC
Chambersburg PA
CBHW051217120626
46547CB00013B/1398

9781966606123